THE NEW CHURCH LADIES

THE **EXTREMELY** UPTIGHT WORLD OF "SOCIAL JUSTICE"

JIM GOAD

OBNOXIOUS BOOKS

Table of Contents

PART I: CRITIQUE

1. The New Church Ladies...2
2. Torch Mobs For Tolerance...5
3. Hating The Haters (In The Name Of Love)...12
4. The Tolerance That Is Only Skin Deep...16
5. How To Deal With The Brainwashed...20
6. How The Free Speech Movement Stopped Moving...25
7. Am I A Racist? Depends On What You Mean By "Racist"...30
8. The Difference Between Prejudice And Postjudice...34
9. Why Is Multiculturalism Necessary?...38
10. Diversity = Division...42
11. Revenge: The Logical Answer To Bullying...46
12. Land Of 1,000 Microaggressions...49
13. Arkansas Store Censors Elton John's Designer Baby!...54
14. White Man Lectures White Girls About Calling Him A "Nigga"...60
15. The Other "N" Word...63
16. The Importance Of Gender-Neutral Public Restrooms For Bisexual Space Aliens...66
17. It's Hard Out Here For A Dudebro...71
18. From Red Scare To Rainbow Scare...75
19. TV Star Loses 70 Pounds, Attacks His Fat Critics, And Gets His Food Show Pulled...78
20. Texas Cheerleader Poses For Photos With Animals She's Killed, Gets Death Threats...81
21. Suey Park, You Are A Fucking Dingbat...85
22. Is It A Hate Crime To Make Fun Of Short People?...88
23. Criticizing PC Totalitarianism—A "90s Thing"?...91
24. The Shame Sham...94

25. My Brief Brush With A Hate-Crime Hoax...*98*

26. Skinheads Against White People...*102*

27. A Blizzard Of Special Snowflakes...*111*

28. Bay Aryan Resistance...*115*

29. A Vast White-Wing Conspiracy...*121*

30. A Handy Guide To Popular Social Justice Hashtags (And What They Really Mean)...*125*

31. What The Hell Do You Mean By "Social Justice," Anyway?...*134*

32. The Social Justice Glossary...*138*

PART II: PARODY

33. I've Finally Realized We Live In A "Rape Culture"...*145*

34. Calling Someone A "Douchebag" Is Hate Speech...*147*

35. 5 Ways To Convert Your Guy Friends Into Feminist Allies...*151*

36. 8 Forgotten Otherkin...*155*

37. The 10 Most Microscopic Microaggressions Of All Time...*159*

38. 8 Geometric Shapes You Didn't Realize Are Problematic...*162*

39. I Told Myself To Stop Whitesplaining But Realized I Was Still Mansplaining...*165*

40. The US Postal Service Is Dominated By White Mails...*168*

41. Judge Orders Hitler To Undergo Therapy...*170*

42. White Man Blames Women, Nonwhites For His Problems...*177*

43. Portland's White Community: Who Are They? Where Are They Going? What Do They Want From Us?...*180*

44. Life Is Unfair, And I'm Here To Change That...*187*

45. Why the Fuck Are There No Gay Drivers In NASCAR?!?...*189*

46. Why Don't They Just Be Honest And Call It "Rapebook"?...*191*

47. Fabricated Hate Crimes By The Transgendered Are Still OK!!!...*193*

48. Sexual Justice Is Never Pleasant...*195*

49. The World's Most Racist Cereal...*197*

50. This White Supremacist Fried Chicken Restaurant In Thailand Is Clearly Unacceptable...*199*

51. They're Already Misgendering The Royal Baby...*201*

52. Watermelon Oreos: A Holocaust For The Metabolism...*203*

53. I Ate a Hamburger—Should I Kill Myself?...*205*

54. Disgusting Fat Asshole Eats Burger, Has Heart
     Attack...*207*

55. Fat Woman's Corpse Sets Building Ablaze During
     Cremation...*209*

56. If You Don't Boycott The All-White Academy Awards,
     You Deserve To Be Shot...*211*

57. I Feel That You Shouldn't Tell Me How I Should Feel
     About My Feelings...*213*

Credits...215

The surest way to work up a crusade in favor of some good cause is to promise people they will have a chance of maltreating someone. To be able to destroy with good conscience, to be able to behave badly and call your bad behavior "righteous indignation"—this is the height of psychological luxury, the most delicious of moral treats.

—Aldous Huxley

Of all tyrannies, a tyranny sincerely exercised for the good of its victims may be the most oppressive. It would be better to live under robber barons than under omnipotent moral busybodies. The robber baron's cruelty may sometimes sleep, his cupidity may at some point be satiated; but those who torment us for our own good will torment us without end for they do so with the approval of their own conscience.

—C. S. Lewis

Political correctness is communist propaganda writ small. In my study of communist societies, I came to the conclusion that the purpose of communist propaganda was not to persuade or convince, nor to inform, but to humiliate; and therefore, the less it corresponded to reality the better. When people are forced to remain silent when they are being told the most obvious lies, or even worse when they are forced to repeat the lies themselves, they lose once and for all their sense of probity. To assent to obvious lies is to co-operate with evil, and in some small way to become evil oneself. One's standing to resist anything is thus eroded, and even destroyed. A society of emasculated liars is easy to control. I think if you examine political correctness, it has the same effect and is intended to.

—Theodore Dalrymple

PART I: CRITIQUE

1

The New Church Ladies

Social-justice warriors, assemble! I'm about to deliver a sermon.

Back in the 1980s—in that Pre-Cambrian era before many of you were even swimming in your dad's scrotum—Dana Carvey on *Saturday Night Live* did a recurring character called "The Church Lady." It was a spot-on parody of a tight-assed, hyper-moralistic Christian woman who was constantly lecturing and demeaning others for their sins.

Now, I don't like Christians any more than you do. But that doesn't mean I'm on your team. As neither a Christian nor a progressive nor a millennial, I have something that most of you lack—perspective. You and the Christians are both wrong about *everything,* and yet you both feel compelled to constantly prove how wrong you are in public.

Although many of you openly mock Christianity and feel you embody its polar opposite, you are incorrect. You are the New Church Ladies.

The sacred secular script you follow—cultural progressivism, egalitarianism, social justice, or whatever the fuck you're calling it these days—is simply Christianity with God removed. Your "God"—your untouchable premise—is the naively childish and entirely unscientific notion of innate human equality. The moralism and the sanctimony and the witch-hunting and the baseless assumptions are exactly the same. Just because your *philosophy* is different doesn't mean your *psychology* is. Your self-righteous mob mentality and communal bloodlust to scapegoat all heretics and burn them at the stake is identical.

Just like church ladies, you have your sins—instead of masturbation and adultery and heresy, they're racism, sexism, and homophobia. You aren't sexually repressed—you're *ideologically* repressed. You still play with your little Angel and Devil figurines just like the Christians do. You flip the characters, but it's the same tired script.

Like the church ladies of yore, you gasp in horror and treat anything that deviates from your Holy Script as blasphemy. You can't bear the idea that people who think differently than you do are allowed to exist. Hence your endless campaigns to shame, silence, and get anyone who deviates from the script fired from their jobs and banished from polite society. Your drive to control and silence all opposition is a religious impulse, not a logical one.

Your thinking is that of a mob, and your shrieking moralism is in many ways indistinguishable to that of fundamentalist Christians. Doesn't your arm get tired from holding that torch all the time?

Shut this down. Erase this. Flag this. This makes me uncomfortable. Give it a trigger warning. This is problematic. Why are you giving this shit a forum? This shit shouldn't exist. Whoever wrote this shit should die. My feelings are hurt. This shit makes me sick. It's disgusting. I'm crying. Give me a pill. I'm calling the cops.

While lecturing me that I walk around with an invisible knapsack of privilege, you walk around with an invisible butt plug of sanctimony. You have moral rectitude lodged firmly up your rectum.

You inhabit a collectivist world of zombie meme-regurgitators for whom "individualism" seems to have become a curse word.

And you implausibly and deceptively label all opposition as fear rather than mere disagreement. Hence your insatiable habit to name and shame a new "-phobia" every week. There's a difference between *disliking* something and being afraid of it, one that flies way over your pious heads.

"Justice" is simply a dishonest word for "revenge." Despite your pretenses of love and compassion, your every word and action reveals you are filled with hate—a *dishonest* hate. I don't have a problem with hate. I hate a lot of things. I *love* to hate. But it's the dishonesty that makes me wish I could vomit in all your faces at once.

Despite the fact that you posture as people who help the little guy, you are backed by the media and the government and the education-industrial complex. You aren't fighting the power; you are the *tools* of power. I can tell where you got fed everything that comes out of your mouth.

Here's the difference between people like me and you: You want to hang me; I don't want to hang *out* with you. Seems as if my approach is less truly hateful and far less intrusive.

But there you go again, dictating what's funny and what's satire and what's acceptable and what's not. Who the fuck died and left *you* Pope?

You're wound so tightly, I can hear you squeaking. For fuck's sake, how self-righteous and hypocritical do you have to get before the mass of us who aren't nearly so self-righteous stand up and start shouting back? The supposedly "intolerant" people have been *way* too tolerant of your endless tantrums.

You are ALWAYS getting offended. You spend every waking moment—and possibly most of your dream life—offended. Jesus Christ, I remember when the young'uns were the LAST to get offended, but now you're the most easily offended people on the fucking planet. Get a grip, you little totalitarians, or the backlash is going to give you diaper rash.

2

Torch Mobs For Tolerance

As I type this from my heavily black neighborhood, I hark back to my wigger days and recall something that Chuck D from black-nationalist rap group Public Enemy said to me wearily when I interviewed him back in 1990:

You tell people what you are, and people still don't believe you.

I couldn't have said it better.

American cultural discourse has imploded with the slimy floridity of a rectal prolapse. At the moment I kinda sorta wish the whole world had one mouth and I could vomit into it.

Still, once again, like Charlie Brown naively rushing up to kick a football that Lucy's holding, I'm going to try to explain myself as well as I can manage, knowing that many of you jerkoffs will misrepresent what I'm saying because, well, that's what jerkoffs do, isn't it?

If you aren't a just another simple, lowly, brainwashed, drearily predictable zombie witch-hunter and sincerely want to understand what makes me tick, the first thing you must accept is that I'm fundamentally antisocial and never, ever, ever, ever, EVER go with the crowd, no matter *what* crowd it is. I figure that wherever the crowd is standing at any given moment, they arrived there for entirely the wrong reasons. Wherever a crowd has gathered, there's never enough space for me. Accordingly, I've had a lifelong affinity for heretics rather than for high priests. The problem is that they keep switching them around, but I always stick with the heretics.

These days, "racist" is the favorite smear word for the ideologically intolerant. I think the term itself is silly and ultimately meaningless, but it's not a word that scares me like it appears to cause testicles to leap out of nutsacks and hit the floor running nationwide. But my interrogators—or, just as often, my accusers—hardly ever seem to be looking for explanations. They don't even seem to know the difference between scientific inquiry and the Spanish Inquisition. Rather, they seem hell-bent on using a rusty knife to pry open my cold heart like a stubborn oyster shell to discover the boundlessly irrational primal HATE they are certain throbs inside. True believers that they are, they take it as an article of faith that evil lurks within the hearts of those who don't think like they do, and goddamnit, they're going to find it whether it's there or not.

There are reasons I choose to live around black people rather than white liberals. For one thing, the rent's cheaper. Another is that I truly and sincerely hate white liberals and couldn't stand to live around them. One day I might even go so far as to write a 15-point guide about how to behave if you should accidentally wander into a white-liberal neighborhood. The blacks tolerate me better, anyway. They have far better senses of humor than white liberals. To them I'm just that Crazy White Boy rather than that Evil White Male. And I think they appreciate and respect that "Crazy" part just enough that they don't fuck with me.

When I was a young outsider I identified with blacks because at the time they, too, were oft-mocked outsiders rather than the untouchable sacred cultural cows into which they've morphed. I'm not impressed with the modern wave of anti-racist whites because there's absolutely no bravery or risk involved with it. I crossed color lines back when there was actually a white herd with a group consciousness in America and most whites would give you flak for doing such things. When I was a fey theater fag in the late 1970s, I invited my half-black cast from an inner-city production of *Godspell* to my birthday party in my all-white neighborhood and caused a minor scandal because of it. There were kids at school who never spoke to me again. In the mid-80s, when it was still somewhat culturally revolutionary for MTV to play Michael Jackson videos, I was the only white guy I knew who had a black girlfriend. By that point in our nation's cultural development, the only people who gave us static about it were black dudes. And I'm still the only white guy I know besides my son who lives in an 87%-black zip code.

Then again, it was a black guy who robbed me at gunpoint in Philly way back in the late 1970s and a black guy who robbed my wife at gunpoint in Atlanta a week after Obama got elected. It was a black guy who punched me in the face in front of a cheering black crowd during a cab dispute in which he was not involved. And I've had more than one black person tell me to my face that I owe them—not for anything I've done, but for, you know, history. So kindly shove your false notions of my sheltered, prejudiced life and lack of real-life experience with blacks somewhere that you don't actually enjoy having them shoved.

Never once have I done or said anything that directly harmed a single black person, yet somehow I'm still made to bear the presumption of eternally indelible inter-generational collective guilt—*talk about a goofball social construct!* And I still don't understand how pointing out such daffily pseudo-religious inconsistencies makes me the worst kind of human being possible rather than someone who calls bullshit when he sees it. If you could explain all that using flow charts and without stooping to name-calling,

I'd be ever so grateful. I, for one, am earnestly searching for explanations rather than for witches. As I see it, pointing this all out doesn't make me a bad person; it makes me a heretic.

It also—ironically, given that we live in a society that gives so much lip service to "diversity"—makes me a heretic to suspect that in aggregate, blacks may truly be different than whites in ways that can be quantified. I think it's preposterous to simultaneously claim to believe in evolution while insisting we all somehow wound up equal. As a believer that the evolutionary process is real and ongoing, I believe their sub-Saharan ancestry may have lent them certain physical advantages and certain cognitive disadvantages.

I know. Horrible, isn't it? How could anyone in this day and age, after all we've been through as a society, believe in what all the evidence suggests and zero evidence disproves? HATE must be the answer; logic has nothing to do with it. Only the unenlightened don't realize this.

I hold this truth to be self-evident: No one is created equal. I also realize that this self-evident truth is so heretical these days, people want to kill you merely for expressing it.

Equality is our modern religion, the glue that holds our shaky social coalition together, and it is never to be questioned. The notion of innate blank-slate human equality must be supported with torch mobs and moral panics and mass delusions and speech codes, because there's nothing—not a shred—in science or logic to support it.

Egalitarianism cannot operate like a science, because there is nothing scientific about it. Since it goes against human nature and biological reality, it eventually must depend on totalitarian tactics in order to sustain itself. In the philosophical realm, it is not supported by logic, so it must operate like a religion instead.

With all this in mind, I have coined two new handy neologisms:

EGALITOTALITARIAN -n 1. One who believes the false concept of equality must be vigilantly enforced by rule of law, whether federal or that of posse comitatus.

EGALIANITY -n. 1. A strict religious system based on the myth that all people are born with equal cognitive and physical qualities.

Every religion needs a Devil, and the Church of Universal Human Equality depends on the utter dehumanization of a stock character called "the racist." This term *used* to mean any white male wearing a brownshirt; these days it signifies any white male who isn't constantly flogging himself while clad in a hairshirt.

The same people who say they're against organized religion are all card-carrying members of the Church of Universal Human Equality, which is perhaps the best organized, most well-funded, and least tolerant mythological system on Earth. I don't even think Islam can compete.

I don't think you anti-racist white witch-hunters wrapped in your golden curtains of righteousness and riding your pale little white ponies hate "racists" so much as you hate heretics. And my guts tell me that 100 years ago, you would have all been in white racist lynch mobs while I would have been the one crazy white guy in town trying to stop you. That's because you are herd animals and I'm forever swimming upstream. Rather than social revolutionaries, way down at the bottom of the tailbone of your souls, you are conformists. Drones. Worker ants. Oooh, how I despise you.

You're right that I have hate in my heart. But you're wrong about the target.

I get along fine with my black neighbors. It's you, Mr. & Mrs. Snarky White Hipster Anti-Racist Witch-Hunter Scooter Club, that I truly hate.

I hate the gross selectivity of your witch-hunting and the fact that you amplify certain racial crimes while blotting others from your collective memory banks.

I hate your movements and your petitions and your boycotts and your perpetually selective outrage. I hate your group shaming, your ritual self-shaming, and the constant status-jockeying that you can only seem to achieve via shaming others.

I hate your endlessly gluttonous lust to punish sinners for committing racism, sexism, and homophobia.

I hate this thing you call "evil" that is always somehow safely quarantined outside of yourself.

I hate the fact that you creeps live your lives with your noses ass-deep in the perceived sins of others.

I hate the primitively moralistic screenplay inside your head where one side is always presumed guilty and the other side is always innocent.

I hate your gross displays of public moral preening.

I hate that you marginalize and dismiss ideas not because they're wrong, but because they don't flatter your herd's self-image.

I hate the fact you've created a climate of fear where things that huge swaths of the public seem to sincerely believe are currently forbidden to even discuss in public forums.

I hate the horrid unreality of your deluded optimism and half-baked utopian schemes.

I hate the special hatred you reserve for those braver than you are.

I hate your arrogant tendency to frame any ideological dissent as a mental-health issue or a cancer of the soul rather than a simple disagreement.

I hate your shallow outrage at people not for saying something that's false, but because they dared to even say it aloud.

I hate your undying obsession with the presumed guilt and turpitude of others.

I hate your strong urge to punish anyone not like you.

I hate that you are only willing to hate what it's socially acceptable to hate.

I hate that you don't even realize you operate like a lynch mob. But you're worse—too chickenshit to do the lynching yourself, you instead enable certain currently endemic forms of racist violence by refusing to acknowledge its very existence.

I hate that I tell you what I am, and you still don't believe me.

May you choke to death on your own smugness.

You silly white-liberal wabbits, always looking for hate in all the wrong places, never realizing that my loathing has almost always been exclusively reserved for you—only you, and you alone.

There—I've explained myself.

Understood? I hope so. Now get off my lawn.

3

Hating The Haters
(In The Name Of
Love)

It's no coincidence that the most flagrantly dehumanizing rhetoric being belched out these days spews from the mouths of those who would likely identify themselves as humanitarians. As proof that much of the modern world is upside-down, most eager practitioners of full-throttle "hate speech"—i.e., speech that pulsates with palpable hatred and anger—are those who'd encourage the silencing or imprisonment of *others* for engaging in "hate speech." Ironically, the loudest practitioners of so-called "hate speech" are those who actually think "hate speech" exists—but only when *someone else* is speaking.

If you see someone online these days being dubbed "a piece of shit," a "scumbag," a "knuckle-dragger," a "Neanderthal," or "subhuman garbage," what's mind-meltingly ironic is that the person who's lobbing these verbal shit-bombs tends to be a liberal—i.e., someone whose entire worldview is based on self-righteous notions of compassion and tolerance. And when you dare call this to their attention, they will call you a subhuman piece of shit merely for pointing out the contradiction between their beliefs and their behavior.

And if you merely note the obvious similarities between their feral, cultish group behavior and that of old-timey lynch mobs, they will call for you to be publicly humiliated and perhaps even physically assaulted. They will say you don't deserve to live and that you and your ilk need to be exterminated—all, but of course, because they think you don't love others in the proper manner.

If they sound like religious fanatics, it's because that's precisely what they are. There is no rational—and definitely no scientific—basis or evidence for a belief that all humans, either as individuals or in terms of average group abilities, are equal. *All* of the evidence suggests precisely the opposite. Since there is not the slightest evidence for human equality, it is nothing more than a belief in a myth that sounds nice and appeals to juvenile emotions. This belief must be swallowed like an invisible Eucharist as an article of faith—and if you do not flow with the crowd and profess faith in that transparently ludicrous premise, you will face the same treatment that heretics have endured throughout history. Their reaction is so fierce and unhinged not because they are so convinced their beliefs are true—no one who's secure in their beliefs would throw such tantrums upon being challenged. Instead, their reactions are those of blind acolytes lashing out at those who question whether their God exists.

This is simply how social psychology works. For any group to form a cohesive identity, they need to define themselves *against* another group, one that is deemed to be inherently inferior. This is known in the emotion-based and highly anti-scientific realm of sociology as the "cultural other." Even though egalitarians blanch at the idea of hating those who aren't like you, they are the most enthusiastic proponents of demonizing the "cultural other" currently playing the game. To many if not most leftists these days, anyone who veers even the slightest from the implausible premise of innate human equality is a caveman throwback who needs to be shat upon before being tarred and feathered and then stoned to death in a public square.

The perceived inferiority of those who don't adhere to the Sacred Creed of Equality need not be biological, although it's telling how often things such as breeding and eugenics infuse the rhetoric of those who don't even claim to believe in eugenics. Merely for disagreeing with them, you will be face-fucked with accusations that you are a genetically deficient inbred mouth-breathing caveman who's on the wrong side of history and will thankfully be bred out of existence. For them, eugenics suddenly becomes hard science when it can be used to portray their ideological opponents as existing several rungs below them on the evolutionary ladder. Anyone who agrees with them is their equal, yet anyone who disagrees is inarguably a lesser human being. This is why the term "scum" is so often used—merely for not embracing their bullshit creed, one is deemed no more evolved than the algae infesting a stagnant pond.

For them, the idea that those who disagree with them are motivated solely by hatred—rather than by the remote possibility that they simply, honestly, and sincerely disagree with them—is enough justification to hate them intensely. They are merely hating the haters in the name of love, so it's not the same thing as hatred. And they actually seem to believe their own bullshit. Such is the blind, self-justifying inhumanity of the modern-day humanist.

I'm often portrayed as an impenitent and irredeemable "hater," and it's true that I hate many elements of human behavior—especially among groups rather than individuals—but I see such character flaws as somewhat equally distributed among all ethnicities and genders and sexual lifestyles. What's hilarious to me is that I don't see anyone on Earth as more or less *human* than I am. Many of them are dumber, for sure. Many of them simply disagree with me. Many of them see the world far differently than I do.

But we're all human, and I've just expressed a more truly humanistic sentiment than anything you'll hear from so-called humanists these days. Tag—*you're* the hater. Hate me if you want—but you know I'm right. Or maybe you don't because you're too fucking dumb to see. But still—you're a hypocrite for hating in the name of love, you fucking hater, you. Not that there's anything wrong with hating *per se*—it's that you look like a clown for not even realizing you bleed hatred from every pore.

4

The Tolerance That Is Only Skin Deep

Country singer George Jones, who to my ears had the greatest voice ever recorded, died in 2013. A genius of phrasing and nuance, Jones had a stratospheric voice that captured human heartbreak with bottomless poignancy. I once read that when Jones was a kid, his father would wake him up in the middle of the night and threaten to beat him if he didn't sing for him. Whether or not that's true, his voice conveyed a tortured soul that was unmistakably human.

The night he died, I was standing outside an Atlanta club where I'd performed an amped-up version of "White Lightning" in honor of Jones's passing. A self-proclaimed fan of mine told me he'd mentioned Ol' Possum's death on Facebook, only to receive a verbal feces-smearing by someone who called Jones a "racist" and a "redneck" who deserves to "rot in hell."

As far as this guy could tell, his Facebook buddy felt Jones's main transgression was that he was a white man who sang country music and was therefore automatically less than human.

Apparently, progressives only believe in hell when their perceived ideological enemies have died, hence the joyous "death parties" when Margaret Thatcher gave up the ghost and the cowardly gloating over Andrew Breitbart's still-warm corpse by sneering, bucktoothed hacks who weren't fit to sniff his underwear.

Without ever feeling a need to apologize, I've done a great deal of hating in my life, but I've never seen a group of twisted, self-satisfied losers so unabashedly hate-filled as modern prog-bots. This is unforgivably and punchably ironic mainly because their entire platform is erected upon shaky Popsicle sticks of "compassion," "tolerance," and respect for the "cultural other." Since their default defense mechanism is to accuse their enemies of being motivated primarily by hatred, it reinforces my belief that the primary impetus of modern leftist psychology is blind, stupid, hypocritical projection.

Just as normal cells mutate into cancer cells and metastasize, the word "liberal" has strayed far from its original moorings and now tends to indicate somehow who despises liberty and freedom and is a pathological control freak that wants to obliterate the mere suggestion of any thought that would undermine their bloated and unwarranted sense of self-worth.

More and more, the modern leftist resembles an 80-year-old film actress who never quite made it in the business and lives huddled somewhere in a dusty Hollywood apartment with 20 cats and five pounds of makeup on her face. Peel away the thick mask she's painted on her crinkled mug, and you have Medusa in curlers.

More and more, it strikes me that leftist compassion is truly skin-deep and goes no further than the epidermis. Oh, sure, they will tolerate a multitude of skin colors (except for the paler manifestations), a sickening array of reconstructive genital mutilations, a Boschian tableau of divergent sex organs crammed into improbable orifices, and any yapping, screaming vagina no matter how hateful or insane the she-beast obviously is.

They will tolerate racial violence as long as the targets are correct. They will applaud homicidal sexism so long as the victims are male. They won't blink if you demean others' sexual orientation so long you're shitting upon the straights. Obviously, their tolerance is massive and ever expanding.

But don't you dare *think* differently than they do. Their tolerance does not extend to what's in your brain.

If you dare to disagree with them, they will attack like a pack of starved rats. Their behavior suggests that they believe others should suffer literally—even corporeally—not because of their actions, but because of their thoughts alone. This will manifest as bald aggression rather than fuzzy compassion. And when *they* mock and threaten, it's not bullying. When they get you fired from your job or reveal your home address, it isn't McCarthyism. When they call you a piece of shit, they aren't dehumanizing you. And when they wish ass cancer upon you, there's nothing hateful about it. They'll engage in purely totalitarian tactics while calling you a fascist.

This is not the behavior of people who are secure in their beliefs. This is the hysterically phobic reaction of those who dread that they might be wrong. If you base everything on a false premise of equality, you'll have to become a liar to keep propping it all up. You'll have to enact codes and laws and punishments for anyone who dares question the sanctity of their fundamental premise.

They demand a rainbow on the outside, but internally, they insist it's all the same dull shade of grey. Their behavior suggests that if they had their way—and through pharmacology and ceaseless propaganda they may one day get it—they wouldn't so much like for everyone to think identically as they'd prefer that everyone share the same brain, an ideological cloud computer that they've meticulously seeded.

Born in 1961, I caught at least two decades of the so-called Red Scare, but what's going on now with political correctness, AKA the bloody afterbirth of the civil-rights movement, is the most egregious moral panic I've seen. This is far more than a battle for the "right" to interracially date or to engage in same-sex *soixante-*

neuf. This goes far deeper than such trivialities. This is a war of attrition to control thought and language and culture, to demean and ostracize anyone who doesn't fall obediently in line, to declare certain subjects beyond discussion and maybe even one day to make it impossible to *think* differently than the herd.

I often wonder what quotient of the population feels effectively silenced. How many Americans fear speaking their minds in the workplace because they don't want to get fired or sued? How many people feel like a pithed frog, mute and helpless, their brain severed from their spine? I suspect that it's quite a few—perhaps even the majority. Although I don't like the feeling, I have a firm sense that it is not me, but rather the whole world around me, that is rapidly going insane. But unlike the modern, deeply indoctrinated, progressive hive-mind robot, I allow the possibility that I could be wrong.

Whereas such ludicrous constructs as Negrophobia, homophobia, and misogyny—which are, by semantic alchemy, presumed never to be the fault of Negroes, homosexuals, or women—are said to be based in a fear of the other or a fear of the unknown, leftist ideological intolerance seems based in a fear of anything that undermines their sacred narrative. At times it seems rooted in a fear that if the threatening idea were to be properly and soberly apprehended, it would invade their consciousness, infect their brains like a virus, and send them into a state of ideological vertigo where they finally realize they are as full of shit as their detractors have always said they are.

So unless you're ready to fight back and never let down, don't ever tell a brainwashed person they're brainwashed. They can handle indoctrination fine, but the truth drives them crazy.

5

How To Deal With
The Brainwashed

I awoke this morning to the creaking sound of the Western mind closing shut. I felt it squeezing in on me like a car crusher. Public discourse is more controlled and political dissent more squashed than at any point in memory. Try as I may, all the evidence suggests we are on the brink of an ideological Dark Age the likes of which America has never seen. It seems we're only inches away from living in a world where stating the obvious will be criminalized.

Online, the chief enablers of this situation are the smirking young social justice warriors, who are unwilling to even touch any viewpoint that hasn't been spoon-fed to them in school or beamed into their eyeballs via TV. Their brains have never hatched a single original idea in their lives. They are mere hollow carriers of infectious ideas, not so much Trojan horses as little pink Trojan ponies.

The modern young leftist is a weak, wretched, psychotic creature, at once nasty and cowardly. Notice how these bespectacled, bearded nerdlings didn't have one shred of bravado until they had the full weight of the government, media, and academia on their side. They are the sort of cowards who were terrified to make a peep until it was absolutely risk-free. They are extremely bold—at least behind a keyboard—until directly confronted when there's no crowd around to protect them. A lone earthworm has more spine than any hundred of them.

Bandwagon-riders that they are, they tell everyone who doesn't think in lockstep with them to "Get with the times," which is a dishonest way of saying, "Be a conformist like I am." Hence their smugness as they tilt at windmills that were destroyed generations ago. They are still deluded that they are fighting the power rather than working for it—often without pay or benefits.

It's one thing to be unwittingly brainwashed, yet quite another to assent to one's brainwashing once it's been made clear. These hateful little fuckers are *defiantly* brainwashed, and whether it's cognitive dissonance or doublethink or pathological lying, they've made it impossible to rationally engage with them. Believe me, I've tried. For decades. Honestly. Foolishly.

It took decades for me to realize I was dealing with fundamentally dishonest people. I naively thought I could politely discuss ideas with people for whom "reason" is a dirty word. But you can't debate the brainwashed. Their cognitive dissonance is too powerful. The truth doesn't matter to them at all. This is why, in nearly all cases, they will flee from the gentlest offer of an earnest discussion. There is to be no debate. There is a reason they won't engage, and it is not because they are certain they are correct. Censors are motivated by insecurity in their own beliefs, but they are not remotely honest enough to admit it.

Their holy cause is all that matters to them, and they feel they've already established—or, rather, declared—that the cause is unassailable. And anyone who challenges the cause must be vilified. So they don't ever engage in debate, only vilification.

To be a modern leftist is to embrace a constellation of lies. They eat lies as if they were corn flakes. Leftism is based on a false premise, and all political systems whose roots are planted in quicksand will inevitably sink into totalitarianism. They start with one flawed premise—equality, which is a laughably obvious lie—and embrace it as an untouchable truth. And they will tell a billion other lies to protect that main lie.

You've heard the lies again and again:

There's a clear line between free speech and hate speech.

Rape has nothing to do with sex.

If you dislike something that we like, you suffer a mental disorder known as a phobia.

Race doesn't exist, but racism is ubiquitous.

Evolution is real, but somehow, inequality isn't.

There is no such thing as an anti-white hate crime or anti-white racism.

Whites are the only group in world history that has ever been ethnocentric.

The nations and peoples who were colonized were peaceful and advanced, and it's not as they would have been colonialists themselves if only they'd had the technology and organizational prowess.

Conformity is a sign of virtue rather than weakness.

Women can't be every bit as nasty and violent as men.

Homosexuality is genetic and has nothing to do with possible childhood sexual trauma.

Children need to be taught to be racist, which is why, um, we spend so much time teaching them not to be racist.

We want equality rather than power.

Two wrongs make a right; in fact, it's known as "justice."

We are open-minded atheistic humanists, which is why anyone who disagrees with us is a subhuman piece of shit who needs to rot in hell.

As the saying goes, the first casualty in war is truth. These little creeps have clearly shown that they feel no compunction to play fair. Leftists are fighting as if they're in a war, and they're acting as if they smell blood. They interpret your fairness as weakness. If you don't even realize that someone has declared war against you,

you're probably going to lose that war. But you can't win a boxing match when your opponent is swinging a mallet.

People who accuse you of being insincere unwittingly reveal a lot about themselves. Same goes for those who accuse you of being hate-filled. Or of being intolerant. Psychological projection is the currency of the hysterical moralist.

People usually play their hand by attacking you with whatever line of attack would work best on them. If their consistent MO is to lob one *ad hominem* Molotov cocktail after another at you, that's a tacit admission that they fear nothing more than public humiliation. By dictating the rules of the game, they unwittingly let you know precisely what it would take to beat them.

They are immune to logic as if they've been vaccinated against it—so go for their emotions. Mock them. *Endlessly* mock them. Publicly mock them. Take their cancerous hatred—which they're openly projecting onto you—and smash them back in the face with it. They're begging for it. They are only being relentless because you've been too nice. Despite how boldly they act, they are obviously horrified of their own shadows.

They're going to call you a "hater" anyway, so you might as well blow off some steam at their expense. Sure, you may have a compulsion to drag them out into the streets and beat them toothless, but that would only validate their fantasies and get you arrested. No, do what they do—only harder. Humiliate them. Publicly. Point out that they are hate-filled, intolerant liars. Toss that bomb right back at them where it belongs.

So many—if not all—of them are obviously reacting against childhood bullying. And even though no one has dared bully them for years, they can't seem to let it go. So bully them back with such soul-crushing gusto, they'll start praying that they were back in high-school gym class. Tie them in pretzel knots made of their emotions.

All it takes to blind them is to hold a mirror in their face. This way they'll know that when confronted, they were the ones who blinked. Never let them forget that. This is why they will hate you far more than they did when they first picked this fight. It is also why you will win.

6

How The Free Speech Movement Stopped Moving

A little over 50 years ago, Mario Savio stood atop a police car at UC Berkeley and gave an impassioned speech to throngs of young pampered radicals that launched what is now preserved in amber and lionized as the "Free Speech Movement." Barefoot and presumably smelly, Savio famously orated something about the "machine"—apparently it was "odious"—and how you had to place your body in the machine's gears to stop it from working.

And in a sense, it worked. But more precisely, the machine only shifted gears. The net result a half-century later on college campuses nationwide is that you are now permitted to say "fuck" but no longer allowed to say "nigger."

In an email forwarded to Berkeley's faculty, staff, and students early in September of this year, school chancellor Nicholas Dirks acknowledged the Free Speech Movement's Golden Anniversary, but with reservations:

...the commitment to free speech and expression can lead to division and divisiveness that undermine a community's foundation....Our capacity to maintain that delicate balance between communal interests and free expression...will be tested anew. Specifically, we can only exercise our right to free speech insofar as we feel safe and respected in doing so, and this in turn requires that people treat each other with civility.

Cutting through that verbal wall of bullshit, Dirks appears to be saying that free speech ends where the "community" begins. He also seems to imply that one person's right to feel "safe and respected" may trump another's right to say what's on their mind.

It is no coincidence that one of the prime movers and shakers of the original Free Speech Movement was Bettina Aptheker, the daughter of dedicated Stalinists and a woman who, despite all the lip service she paid to "free speech," openly supported thought-squashing socialist regimes throughout the 1960s, the sort of tyrannical state entities that would rip your tongue out of your throat for making the merest bird squeak of dissent. Aptheker is now a professor of feminist studies at UC Santa Cruz and recently wrote this in a Berkeley alumni magazine:

On the occasion of this 50th anniversary of the FSM...it is worth pausing for a moment to consider the ways in which gender, race, class, and sexuality may effect [sic] one's access to freedom of speech. Although the First Amendment embraces a universal ideal in its wording, it was written by white, propertied men in the 18th century....

Lady, if I was against free speech, I'd tell you to shut the hell up right now. But I'll let you prattle onward and downward, because you're only proving my point.

What a despicable group of tyrants the freewheeling leftists of the early 1960s have become. Those who rose up against the "machine" back then are still working from the old operator's manual. Miraculously, they still manage to convince themselves that they have not *become* the machine against which they once railed. And somewhere along the line they concocted the screwball idea of "hate speech"—I doubt such a concept so much as existed in 1964—and began fallaciously arguing that it was a fundamentally different thing from free speech. They spun a magical illusory world where "civil rights" and "civil liberties" are somehow at odds with one another. They even convinced untold numbers of otherwise intelligent people that if you stopped calling blacks dirty names, those benighted and oppressed descendants of slaves would perform better academically.

They *still* whine about McCarthyism, which would be fine if they were able to point to a single Nazi screenwriter currently employed in Hollywood. In their childish quest to avoid creating a "hostile environment," they've engineered an environment that is brutally hostile to the merest wisp of dissent. They have engineered a coddled, over-medicated world where mild disapproval of anything is "hate speech." In the service of "sensitivity," they have fashioned a modern educational system that is an uninterrupted blood libel against white males. They have achieved ethnic, gender, and sexual diversity—at the almost complete expense of ideological diversity. It is a world where feelings overrule ideas at every turn. Ideas—at least ones that diverge a millimeter from official indoctrination—are viewed as threats.

The mind of a censor is a dark and frightened space. Censors are motivated not by a certainty that their targets are wrong but a fear that they may be right. The end result of the Free Speech Movement has been to create a generation of graduates whose minds are bolted shut and paved over with cement.

In the interest of delusional and unquantifiable intangibles such as "equality" and "social justice," the totalitarian wolves in free-speech clothing who arose in Berkeley fifty years ago have created a suffocating environment that is more hostile to the free exchange of ideas than perhaps at any time in American history.

They've fostered a savagely intolerant climate where the president of Harvard can get canned merely for suggesting that the sexes may be different. Where someone who uses the evil patriarchal tool of mathematics to deflate overblown hysteria about sexual assault on campus is disinvited from a campus speaking engagement. Where Yale students are prevented from quoting F. Scott Fitzgerald due to the imagined "homophobia" in the word "sissies." Where displaying "a condescending sex-based attitude towards a person" constitutes sexual harassment. Where merely uttering "sexist statements" is deemed a literal *act* of sexual harassment. Where you can be prohibited from using computers to transmit "material, which in the sole judgment of the University is offensive, violent, pornographic, annoying or harassing...." Where students are confronted by campus police for—get this—merely handing out copies of the US Constitution.

Colleges have become indoctrination factories where incoming students are instructed that all whites are racists and that nonwhites are incapable of racism. Where freshmen—sorry, *freshpersons*—at Harvard were asked to sign an oath affirming the highly anti-intellectual notion that "kindness holds a place on par with intellectual attainment." Where any guest speaker, no matter how reasonable or genteel, can be shouted off a campus by infantile mobs of pampered leftists who only differ from students at Berkeley in the early 1960s in the sense that their actions are now utterly risk-free.

This has had more than a mere "chilling effect" on free speech. In many cases, it has absolutely frozen the possibility of open debate. A wide-ranging 2010 study revealed that a mere 35.6% of college students "strongly" agreed it is "safe to hold unpopular positions on campus." Among faculty and staff, it was even worse—a piddling 18.5% agreed with that statement.

If any of the ideological descendants of the original Free Speech Movement gave a fig about free speech, they'd stop the ritual silencing, shaming, and expulsion of anyone who doesn't kowtow to predatory egalitarianism and incessantly ludicrous leftist pieties.

The repression is hardly confined to campuses, although that's where it originated and remains most intense. It is also rampant in the media, in the workplace, and online. Things are so repressed that the vast majority of online commenters who don't toe the dominant ideological line are wary of using their real names for fear of the consequences. This is a climate that is anything but free. It is high time to throw our bodies full-force on this new, smiley-faced machine that seeks to crush us.

7

Am I A Racist? Depends On What You Mean By "Racist"

When people ask me if I'm a "racist"—which seems to be daily—I never say "yes" or "no" without first asking them what they mean by the term.

This flummoxes them, because they assume the word "racist" has some sort of fixed socio-scientific meaning, that there's an easy "yes" or "no" answer, and that nobody would ever willingly answer "yes."

Even though they insist "race"—i.e., quantifiably different physical and cognitive patterns between groups of different continental origins—doesn't exist, they act as if the definition of "racism" is fixed in cement.

Sorry to pop your One-World Love Bubble, but "race" is far easier to quantify than "racism." A forensic scientist could take

DNA samples from a skull and determine its continental origins, but they would be utterly incapable of telling you whether the skull once harbored "racist" thoughts. The true "social construct" here is "racism," not "race."

Problem is, the definition of the word "racist" has evolved...or devolved...or, more accurately, ballooned...over the course of my lifetime.

So when I calmly—*cheerfully*, even—ask them to define the term "racist," it stymies them because they think it's the worst thing in the world to be a racist and that everyone would automatically deny being one. And for many modern-day simpletons who'd be incapable of squeezing an original thought out of their head if you held a gun to it, denying that you're a racist is the surest proof that you're a racist. They also expect you to scramble to prove that you aren't a racist, such as offering up evidence that you have black friends or listen to hip-hop or once ate some watermelon. No matter what you say, if they want to think of you as a racist, they're going to do it. It has less to do with your actual beliefs and far more to do with their self-righteousness and conformist personality. This childish, hysterical, torch-carrying, witch-hunting mentality has truly become that stupid and histrionic.

But nasty scare words don't cow me like they appear to terrify others. When a person is OK with himself, the approval or condemnation of others doesn't mean a thing. Then again, the problem with being an individual is that you always wind up outnumbered.

It used to be that a "racist" was simply someone who hated others for their skin color. By that definition, I am not, nor have I ever been, a racist. People give you plenty of reasons to hate them before you even have to consider their melanin levels. Most people I've hated have been white—especially the ones who play an infantile, morally hierarchical, status-jockeying game of "tag" by calling me a racist.

When I was much younger, the word "racist" had the same

sinister implications it does now, only it was confined to those who had actual sinister motives or who engaged in sinister acts. I have never wanted to harm anyone because they had a different ancestry than I did. I've wanted to harm *plenty* of people because of their behavior, but never because their ancestry was different than mine. So according to that definition, nope, I'm still not a racist.

Another common idea of what constitutes a "racist" is someone who scapegoats other races for their problems. Nah, that's not me. I blame my parents and, increasingly, myself. So by that definition, I am not a racist.

One also hears that a "racist" is one who, because of deep-seated feelings of inadequacy, needs to feel that their race is superior to others. I may have intense feelings of superiority about certain things, but they have nothing to do with my skin color or continental ancestry. By most physical measures, I'd say that blacks are superior to whites. By most known cognitive indices, Asians and Jews are superior to whites. So because I do not base my superiority complex on being white, I am not a racist according to that definition.

But increasingly, a "racist" is someone who dares to even notice general patterns of difference among groups of different continental origins. I stress the terms "general patterns" and "different continental origins" because a semantic trick some people play is to insist that no race is "pure" and therefore race is a meaningless term, but I've never suggested this "purity" concept and I'm not sure that anyone has. To deny that Kenyans are generally better long-distance runners than Samoans, or that Japanese students consistently score higher than Australian aborigines on intelligence tests, or that Germans have contributed more to science than Guatemalans, is to deny reality. So if noticing patterns makes me a racist, then yes—absolutely. I am a racist—a shameless one, too. I have no shame in following what the overwhelming evidence suggests. If you can show me contrary evidence, I'll consider it—but you'd be far more persuasive if you stopped shouting and calling me naughty names in the process. It only makes you, not me, look like the hater.

Finally, it's becoming evident that a "racist" is any white person who doesn't publicly flog themselves for being white, who doesn't ignore the tremendous contributions of European civilization to world history, who filters out all the good and only focuses on genocide and hatred and oppression, as if every other civilization didn't own slaves and demonize the "other" and slaughter all enemies to the best of their ability. By this definition, a "racist" is any white person who wouldn't crawl out of their white skin if given the opportunity. As I see it, self-hatred is not an appealing trait in any individual or any group. It wasn't attractive in blacks when they were shuffling and muttering "Yes, massa," and it's extremely unbecoming in whites when they're constantly apologizing for their very existence. So if merely being unashamed—not *proud*, that's an entirely different thing—of being white makes me a racist, then I am an unreconstructed, unapologetic R-A-C-I-S-T, and you can kiss my lily-white ass if you don't like it.

8

The Difference
Between Prejudice
And Postjudice

"Prejudice" is a loaded and deceptive word, because it implies that if you were only to spend enough time around a given group of people, you'd love the hell out of them. It also implies that you'd stop stereotyping them rather than start noticing patterns among them.

The word is derived from a Latin compound meaning "prior judgment"—in other words, making a decision about a subject without sufficient exposure to the thing you're judging. And as the term is usually employed, you're judging it negatively rather than positively. If a white person is said to be prejudiced against blacks—and that's usually how it goes, because I can't ever remember hearing that a black person is "prejudiced" against whites—the implication is that they've developed an irrational fear and hatred of them due to a lack of real-life contact with them. They are *pre*-judging them without enough experience to cast a reasonable judgment.

Gordon Allport's landmark 1954 book *The Nature of Prejudice* gave rise to what is known as "contact theory," which again implies that if you were merely to rub elbows enough with a group of people who are fundamentally different than you are, all your fears would melt away and you wouldn't begin realizing that on average, they behave differently, hold different values, and perhaps even possess different cognitive and physical attributes than you do.

I use the term "on average" because it's crucial. An exception may disprove an ironclad rule, but it does not entirely erase demonstrable statistical patterns. Every once in a while you'll find a great Chinese basketball player, but that's not the general pattern. Every so often I'll run across a dumb Jewish person, but overall, Jews excel in academic endeavors far beyond their numbers. There are exceptions to every stereotype, whether positive or negative. But there are also observable patterns that gave rise to the stereotypes in the first place.

Two Indian boys recently tied for first place in the Scripps National Spelling Bee. It marked the seventh straight year that Indian-Americans came in first. Seeing as how Americans of Indian ancestry comprise only 1% of the population, the odds that Indian-Americans would win for seven straight years are somewhere around 1 in 100 trillion. Considering that two of them won this year, that makes eight straight Indian-Americans doing better than every other American child. If one had zero preconceived notions that any ethnic group was better than any other one at spelling—in other words, if one was, without any evidence, *prejudiced* to believe that everyone is equal at spelling—the odds that eight Indian-Americans in a row would win are a staggering 1 in 10,000,000,000,000,000.

So regarding Indian-Americans and spelling, I am not prejudiced about the fact that on average, they are great at it. I am *postju-*

diced about it. I have reviewed the evidence and made a judgment *afterward*, not before it.

Many of you would claim that black people have every right to dislike and be suspicious of white people. But is that due to a *lack* of contact with them? No, you'd probably argue that it's due to *hundreds of years* of contact with them. Therefore, many blacks are postjudiced regarding white people. They're judging from experience, not lack of experience.

As a Philly cabdriver for years, I had plenty of black customers. In total over those years, I was tipped one dollar by black people. Even the black cabdrivers would complain about how black customers don't tip. I know several people who work in the service industry, particularly restaurants, and they all have the same complaint—although there are exceptions, black people tip very poorly on average. Many of these people became waiters and waitresses with no preconceived notions—no prejudices—about how blacks might tip. Their pattern-recognition came from experience, so it constituted postjudice rather than prejudice. There's even a study from Cornell University that lends support to this stereotype.

I'm constantly bemused with how much shit-talking and moral finger-pointing that white people from, say, an "enlightened" town such as Seattle do about those horrible "racist" white Southerners. But Seattle is only 8% black; Mississippi is 37% black. Historically, the South has always been the blackest part of the United States. More than half of black Americans still live in the South. So who really has had more contact with black people—snooty white progs in Seattle, or those perpetually demonized Southern rednecks? Who truly is prejudging here?

What if, say, you moved to Chile with no preconceived notions about how Chileans act, yet you had one horrible experience with them after the next for years and years until you decided to leave? Should you put blinders on, shut off what your brain is telling you, play an ethnic game of "The Emperor's New Clothes," and pretend that on average, you actually *like* Chileans?

Only if you're a sissy who's more afraid of social disapproval than you are of listening to your heart. (I'm only picking a country at random, so sit down and quit getting so excited. For all I know, Chileans could be wonderful people. I haven't met enough of them to judge.)

And this is one of the grand problems with the escalating insanity about this phantom, elusive, and ultimately unattainable ideal known as "equality"—it denies essential differences between people. It also denies people the right to develop their own tastes and distastes based on their personal experiences.

Is it dumb to form broad, blanket assumptions about people you've never met? Absolutely. Is it dumb to make generalizations about people after you've had extensive contact with them, even allowing that there are exceptions to general patterns? No—it's called "noticing." And therein lies the difference between prejudice and postjudice.

9

Why Is Multiculturalism Necessary?

Why do people who shout the loudest about multiculturalism's glories all seem to look, think, talk, and act the same? And if they truly believe that all cultures and races and genders are equal, why do they never shut the fuck up about how horrible and worthless straight white males are?

Usually under the excuse that something is "too white," we hear that it needs to diversify, and, like, fucking PRONTO.

We don't hear that hip-hop is too black.

We don't hear that nail salons are too female.

We don't hear that baseball is too Latin American.

We don't hear that taco trucks are too Mexican.

We don't hear that horse jockeys are too short.

We don't hear that San Francisco is too gay or that Portland is too lesbian.

We don't hear that China is too Chinese or that Africa is too black or that New York and Hollywood are too Jewish.

We only hear that things are too white, too male, or too hetero. And the moment that any white hetero male has the guts to make a peep about it, out you come tut-tutting and attempting to shame like some frigid postmenopausal nun.

Since the endless shrieking cant is that white males are a problem, you shouldn't be surprised if white males begin to object. And if you keep shouting down and attempting to punish white males merely for questioning your true agenda and endlessly demonizing the very idea of white males' existence, don't start crying if you eventually create a backlash that blows your face off. Self-hatred is not attractive in anyone. Neither is abject submission to endless insults and demonizing. Have you noticed that the more that white males acquiesce to your endlessly holier-than-thou shame tactics, the more they get mocked? This is not an accident. This is because no one respects the self-loathing. It's a natural animal instinct that if someone bends over, you fuck them.

If you have the remotest understanding of history beyond TV movies, you'd know about the Moors and Hannibal and Genghis Khan and Islamic invasions...in short, you'd know that white male Europeans were hardly the only aggressors.

Of the alleged oppressed groups, though they may give lip service to "diversity," in practice they're usually griping that any given profession or area isn't black, Mexican, or gay ENOUGH. They don't seem to want it MORE diverse; they simply want more power for their own group.

Don't get me wrong, *kemosabe*. I actually like diversity, and not merely in the typically understood sense that it's handy for sheltered upper-middle class zombie whites because it gives them a wide selection of restaurants in neighborhoods that most members of the other cultures that are ostensibly being "celebrated" could never afford to live in the first place. I like learning about other religions, other languages, other music, other philosophies, and other traditions. But cramming them all together into smaller and smaller spaces isn't going to create diversity. It'll create conflict, endless hierarchical bitching about "rights" and who wins the Gold Medal for oppression, and, worst of all—if anyone survives the conflict—it'll create uniformity. It'll actually destroy diversity.

Wiping out freedom of association will also wipe out diversity. If you only want to associate with people who are over seven feet tall, why the fuck should anyone else care? If an employer wants to hire only Filipino lesbians, why the frickety-frack is that anyone else's business besides the employer's? Yes, I realize it's against the law to discriminate. On average, it's also against the law not to work from January 1 to late April just to pay the government the lunch money that those bullies demand from you under threat of imprisonment. It also used to be against the law for women and blacks to vote. There are literally millions of stupid laws. I'm pretty sure it's still illegal to eat pussy in several states. The law is not always right. The law is probably far more often used to oppress than it is to free the oppressed. The phrase "No one is above the law" implies that humans are beneath the law. The law doesn't give rights, it only takes them away. The law, for the most part, exists to make lawyers rich.

A supposedly "tolerant" world is being created where, ironically, everyone's nose is up everyone else's ass. And more and more, you aren't allowed to choose whose ass your nose goes up and whose nose goes up your ass. These choices aren't being made *by* you; they're being made *for* you.

It's not diversity. It's conformity. And it's not multiculturalism. It's the forced imposition of a monoculture for what I suspect are largely financial reasons by insanely greedy control freaks.

To truly honor diversity, you have to honor the wish of some individuals and groups to remain separate. But that doesn't seem to be what this endless globalist onslaught is about. It's about centralizing power. Multiculturalism appears necessary only to erase borders in the service of creating a global labor pool. It appears necessary only to create a global economy for a tiny handful of international financiers to plunder at the expense of the many.

Forcibly herding everyone together—the black sheep, the white sheep, the yellow sheep, and the pink sheep—without borders, without boundaries, and without tolerance for ideological dissent—is going to create only one culture, not a multiplicity of them. Instead of acknowledging and honoring differences, it's going to erase them. Eventually, it will also eliminate genetic diversity. And that's not a rainbow. It's a cloudy, drizzly day.

I understand that technology is making the world smaller and smaller. I also suspect it's making the world more and more similar. It's actually killing diversity rather than preserving or "celebrating" it. It will, in the end, erase cultural diversity and give us a stultifyingly bland cultural uniformity. It will mean people of many skin colors and languages and sexual lifestyles will all shop together at McDonald's and Home Depot.

It also appears to be a zero-sum game in the sense that the more racially, religiously, and sexually diverse a society you attempt to construct, the more you demand ideological conformity and the less you tolerate anyone who dares to entertain a different way of thinking...like, for example, daring to think that this bold and vibrant "diversity" that one must never question without ostracism, career death, physical threats or assaults—and in some European countries, even jail time, as sick and Orwellian as that is—might not exactly be this shimmeringly benign entity that it's being peddled as. It is, in fact, only a new form of colonialism. And if it gets its way, it will be the final form of colonialism.

Busting up the Tower of Babel was the best idea the fictional biblical God ever had.

10

Diversity = Division

Much of the public has unquestioningly embraced the mantra "Diversity is Strength." Then again, in George Orwell's dystopian novel 1984, much of the public also blindly accepted oxymoronic slogans such as "WAR IS PEACE" and "FREEDOM IS SLAVERY." Throughout history, the general public has been little more than a giant hardware store full of tools.

A Google Images search of the word "diversity" shows an uninterrupted syrupy stream of rainbows and smiling faces and clasped hands, a global clog dance where everyone gets along because that's naturally what occurs whenever you cram people of different continental origins, religions, languages, and ideologies together in the same space...right?

I mean, if that's accepted as the sort of common wisdom that you can't dare question without being branded a witch, that's what the historical record would show...*n'est-ce pas?*

According to the Online Etymology Dictionary, the word "diversity" only acquired a positive connotation regarding things such as race and gender in 1992. Prior to that, the word was derived from the French word *diversité*, which signified less cheery synonyms such as "wickedness" and "perversity" and the ancient Latin word *diversitatem*, which connoted "contrariety, contradiction, [and] disagreement."

It's instructive that the modern word "diversity" is rooted in a Latin word that signified "disagreement." Perhaps the primary reason the Roman Empire crumbled was because it spread itself too thin and allowed incursions from non-Roman ethnic elements. Diversity's weight proved too much for the empire to sustain itself.

Note the similarity between the words "diversity" and "division," the latter of which is derived from "divide." Fifteenth-century Italian political strategist Niccolò Machiavelli posited a basic rule of politics: *"divide et impera,"* which in English is most often translated as "divide and conquer."

India is often said to be the most diverse country on Earth. And diversity worked so well there that its eastern and western provinces split off into Pakistan and Bangladesh amid oceans of blood.

According to the map in a *Daily Mail* article titled "Worlds Apart," Africa is the most ethnically diverse continent on Earth, yet it continues to eat itself alive due to ongoing tribal conflicts that may have been *exploited* by colonialists but that existed long before Europeans ever set foot in Africa and have persisted—and even escalated—once the colonialists began their slow retreat.

European history is replete with homicidal group conflicts that may on their surface appear to have been rooted in religion or ideology but were more deeply entwined with things such as cultural, linguistic, and phenotypical differences.

For all the badmouthing that the American South gets for being "racist," it is no coincidence that it has always been the *least* uniformly white part of the United States. For racism to exist at all, you sort of need more than one race to get the fire started.

So rather than the rainbow fantasies and bubblegum dreams that are endlessly peddled by the world's power-hungry would-be central planners, the historical record tends to show that instead of harmony, ethnic diversity leads to ethnic conflict. To blindly chant "celebrate diversity" is akin to chanting "celebrate conflict."

Or maybe that's giving the globalists too much credit—if they aren't being purposely manipulative, then they are hopelessly naïve.

After Obama was elected, the "post-racial" society we were promised did not emerge. If anything, things got *more* racial. Instead of everyone getting *over* race, they grew increasingly obsessed with the topic. People aren't *celebrating* differences, they're *highlighting* them. Instead of harmony, we have endless infantile pissing matches over status and hierarchy and the depressingly persistent primitive religious notion of historical collective guilt.

As this new consensus nation that was hastily stitched together into a patchwork quilt struggles to define itself, it is hardly inclusive—for reasons of social psychology that an antisocial person such as myself can't emotionally grasp, all in-groups appear to need an out-group, so the script was flipped and the new Devil became white people, specifically the all-consuming Beelzebub pejoratively referred to as the "white male."

Here's a radical idea, and I know this makes me an impenitent hatemonger: Although I believe the evidence suggests that many physical and cognitive traits may be hereditary, I doubt that *character* is genetic at all. I believe all human beings, both individually and in groups, have a more or less equal potential to be assholes. If given the chance, they also have an equal potential to be noble.

If you continue to scratch your head and wonder why many white males aren't down with your program, perhaps you should quit ceaselessly smearing shit in their faces. Otherwise, considering the historical lessons, you're begging for conflict rather than harmony, and you may be hastening a rather nasty pushback.

I honestly don't know if there's an easy way out of this mess. If I ever figure it out, I'll let you know. It may be possible, but Jesus Christ, you're going about it all wrong. If you keep playing your juvenile game of Devils & Angels, Americans will *never* get along with one another. EVERYONE needs to lighten the fuck up, and instead of what the innately humorless social-justice zombies would dictate, we need MORE racial jokes rather than fewer ones. If Americans can't learn to laugh at their differences rather than consistently generate increasingly oppressive taboos in thought and speech, the entire nation will go absolutely fucking insane. We'll have a rainbow world where everyone is clasping hands so hard that their knuckles bleed, where they're forcing their smiles to the point where their faces crack into pieces and fall to the ground.

Ethnic, cultural, and linguistic diversity may ultimately mean we might never get along—at least not entirely—but the worst possible solution would be to cut off everyone's tongues. If you're really sincere about the idea that diversity is a good thing, you need to quit insisting that everyone should THINK exactly like you do. Unanimity of thought—especially when it's enforced through speech codes and laws that restrict and criminalize ideological dissent—is not tolerance, it's totalitarianism. Tolerating different ideas is the most important form of tolerance.

Despite what you may wish, I honestly couldn't give a fuck about your skin color, gender, or what you do with your genitals. And unlike many of you—perhaps the majority—I can tolerate the idea that you may think differently than I do. But if you want to demonize me for *my* skin color or the fact that I don't follow the script that you've eagerly swallowed like a baby bird being fed a worm, I think we know who the bigot is in this equation.

11

Revenge: The Logical Answer To Bullying

One of the most consistently puzzling things to me about latter-day social-justice lynch mobs is their innate meanness and viciousness, since their entire philosophy is predicated on the idea that they are the underdogs who are fighting the bullies. But that's patently untrue, as it's obvious that they now have the social and political weight on their side.

I've always been amused but perplexed at how much seething hate is hurled these days at the alleged "haters," whether they be "racists," "sexists," or "homophobes." The ones who get banished from the herd with extreme prejudice and hatred are the bullies of *yesteryear*, not of today. If you objectively scrutinize what's being said and done, far more vitriol and dehumanizing rhetoric flows from the self-righteous mouths of those who claim to be fighting "hate." The most flagrantly hateful people of the past few years—in both words and actions—do it in the name of love and compassion and basic human decency. Ironically, the purported "haters" are relatively tame compared to those who are attacking them.

What this says to me is that all of these superficially innocent social struggles have never really been about equality—they've been about winning. Their main goals, consciously or at least instinctually, have not been to foster harmony but to establish new social pecking orders. In a very weird and depressing way, it seems that although the good guys and bad guys may change costumes, the haters and bullies always win. Apparently, that's nature's way. In the long run, despite the lip service they may pay to fighting for the underdog, people would rather come out on top. Judging strictly from their behavior instead of what they say, they'd rather be hypocrites than unhealthy.

If you are one of the millions of bullying victims in the United States who hides in the shadows eating three square meals of shame daily, I have some advice for you. I don't want you to tell your parents. I don't want you to tell your teacher. I don't want you to call the cops. Doing any of those things only makes you look like a pussy.

I want you to bully *back*.

I want you to retaliate with such unhinged, violently psychotic, Viking-thunderbolt vengeance that your bully is placed in a constant crippling fear of the fact that you still exist on this planet. I want him to shit his pants at the very thought of you.

Make him realize that fucking with you is just not worth it, that you will take it further than he'd ever dare, that even though he may be a little crazy, you are a seventh-degree black belt in crazy.

It's the only logical way to stop them. It's easily the most effective. If you allow yourself the pleasures of sadism from time to time, it can also be insanely gratifying.

Your bully may have stolen your lunch money. But he's going to have trouble chewing his bologna sandwich after you threw that beaker of sulfuric acid in his face.

Your bully may be bigger and stronger than you are. But can he stop a car that's headed at 80MPH right for his kneecaps?

Your bully may make fun of your mild acne problem. That'll be a lot harder to do once he's confined to an iron lung.

Your bully may scoff at your sexuality. But can his immune system withstand the AIDS virus once it's been jabbed into his ass with a dirty needle in the hallway between classes while he's leaning on a locker talking to some chicks?

Someone's harassing your handicapped cousin? Make it so that asshole has to eat through a straw for the rest of their life and can only communicate by blinking their left eyelash.

Jesus said to turn the other cheek, and look what happened to *him*. No, if a man striketh you on the cheek, you *remove* both of his cheeks. Using ice tongs. And a blowtorch. While reciting the 23rd Psalm.

Of course, don't do anything illegal, because that would be stupid.

12

Land Of 1,000 Microaggressions

If a person of color feels offended by something a well-meaning white person said and no one knows they're offended, is it still a hate crime?

This is the implicit question posed by the very idea of "racial microaggressions." The concept seems to have been formulated by the racial-grievance industry to fill the savage dearth of truly aggressive acts committed by whites toward nonwhites over the past few generations.

In other words, if what used to be known as "racism" no longer exists, you have to greatly expand the term's breadth so that it includes words, thoughts, and acts that have zero conscious hostility behind them. You have to make everything racist just to stay in business.

The term "microaggression" was allegedly coined by Harvard professor Chester M. Pierce in 1970 to describe rude or dismissive behavior he claims to have seen evil whites routinely inflicting on innocent blacks. In 1973 a female economist at MIT named Mary

Row hijacked Pierce's neologism and expanded it to include the endless perceived slights, insults, and random cruelties that so many women claim to experience whether others realize it or not.

But it was Columbia psychology professor Derald Wing Sue—an Asian male in case such things are important to you—who really took the concept of "microaggressions" to the hoop in 2007 when he broke it down further into four micro-categories. This boy named Sue distinguished between "microassaults," "microinsults," "microinvalidations," and, most amusingly, "microrape."

According to Wikipedia, microrape is "Characterized by predatory non-physical prurient communications with the intent to penetrate the victim's emotional security on the basis of hetero-normative impositions."

A handy table from the University of Wisconsin outlines several prominent forms of racial microaggressions. These include asking a person where they were born, assuming an Asian person is adept at math, and making seemingly benign (if undeniably sappy) comments such as "There is only one race, the human race." The table also insists that if you say the best-qualified person should get the job, your soul bears the ineffable stain of having committed a racial microaggression.

Even if you have no hatred in your heart for a person of color and even if you make the most obsequious gestures of appeasement toward them, you are still hurting them and acting racist toward them because, well, you're white, and that's what you people do.

That's what's ultimately dangerous about this concept of "microaggresions"—even the demented fanatics who insist that such things actually exist will concede that the perpetrator may not harbor or exhibit any malice whatsoever. They may not even be the least bit conscious that they are being horrid bigots. Under this framework, bigotry is solely in the eyes of the accuser. No matter how pleasant your demeanor or how generously you act, you can still be bludgeoned over the head with baseless accusations of unconscious racism, and your accuser will feel like a good person for doing it.

I can't imagine the agony of being a person of color on a college campus these days, what with all the microaggressions, microinsults, microinvalidations, microassaults, and especially all the microrape. Why, it's enough to make a person of color want to drop out of college entirely.

In fact, a recently released study about racial microaggressions seems to blame these invisible, unintentional acts of racism for the relatively high dropout rates and low academic performance among a certain racial group who shall not be named but you can probably guess anyway which is why I don't feel the need to name them, which I suspect may be my unconscious way of racially microaggressing upon them, which is kinda interesting if you're able to stop and think about it all without your head exploding.

The study bears the catchy title of *Racial microaggressions at the University of Illinois at Urbana-Champaign: Voices of students of color in the classroom.* I highly recommend it as the finest comedic document I've seen so far this year.

Sponsored by the University of Illinois Racial Microaggressions Project and conducted by a specially appointed "Racial Microaggressions Team" whose associates have colorful first names such as Efadul, Shinwoo, Tanisha, Sang, and Artesha, the study concludes that it really, really, really, *really* sucks to be a person of color on campus these days.

For example, a robust two-fifths of the online study's respondents claimed they "felt uncomfortable on campus because of their race." All I can do is shake my head and softly mutter, "Must suck to be them."

Some sample testimonials from the POCs who claim to have been microaggressed upon:

People do not necessarily say I do not belong, but I feel as if I do not when I am in a classroom and I am the one non-White person. (Latina, Female)

I was in a class and mentioned that I had visited South Asia a few months back. After I mentioned that, the professor immediately asked me if I had ever ridden an elephant only because I was from South Asia. I was not necessarily insulted, but I did feel it was a really stereotypical question to ask and she asked me in front of the entire class. I thought it was rude. (Asian, Female)

When I raise my hand, I am often not called upon. After a while, I found myself refraining from asking questions. (African American, Male)

When will such hatred end? What year is this again? Isn't this why we fought the Civil War and, um, Hitler? Didn't everyone start smoking dope and throwing rocks at cops back in the 1960s just so that fifty years later, paranoid Latina females can imagine that white students are silently hating them even though these gringos haven't done the slightest thing to suggest such a thing?

According to the study's authors, certain snooty white classmates said that nonwhites who complained about microaggressions were merely whiny babies that were "angry," "overreacting," or "defensive." The authors say that such accusations constitute yet "another racial microaggression" committed by the startlingly impenitent whites.

Sure, it may not seem like much—or, more reasonably, it may seem like nothing at all—but the authors claim that cumulatively, such microaggressions inflict severe harm upon the hapless nonwhite students of the University of Illinois. Suffering such constant invisible psychic needling invariably causes students of color to endure "fear, resentment, helplessness, isolation, stress and exhaustion." It can also lead to "physical symptoms such as, [sic] headaches, high blood pressure, and fatigue."

To remedy these imaginary torments and tortures, the study's authors recommend that all students be forced to "complete a General Education requirement about race, White privilege, and inequality in the United States." They "must take both a non-Western culture and a US people of color cultural course," too. Not only that, the university system should "Include diversity and inclusion in a third of the curriculum of all college 101 classes."

And really, who besides an incurable bigot would be against including inclusion? Why do we even need to teach anyone math and logic when we can just keep telling them that white people are assholes?

I sincerely doubt that "racial microaggressions" against non-whites are a problem on American college campuses. It seems like these days, most white people would rather slit their own throats than be accused of racism. The more likely scenario is that idiotic concepts such as "racial microaggressions" comprise an ongoing act of passive-aggression toward white people. And there's nothing "micro" about it. Instead, it's right out there in the open.

13

Arkansas Store Censors Elton John's Designer Baby!

A global scandal erupted in 2011 after someone complained about the manner in which a grocery store in Mountain Home, Arkansas was displaying an *Us Weekly* cover featuring sextuagenarian songbird Elton John, his widow-peaked "partner" of 17 years David Furnish, and their month-old bioengineered son Zachary Jackson Levon Furnish-John—who may or may not be gay, nor, as far as I can tell from that cover photo, even alive.

After spotting the magazine on display at a Harps regional grocery-chain outlet, a local Arkansas native Tweeted that she was "shocked" and "horrified" at what she'd seen and publicly inquired whether anything could possibly be done to rectify this clearly unacceptable and morally abhorrent situation.

The story soon went viral, along with the sad, predictably

uptight bleatings of pharisaical outrage among faceless, small-minded commenters:

> "[W]e're still horrified that this even happened in the first place...offensive...disgraceful...appaling [sic]...twisted...wrong...outrageous."

Many of the comments crossed the line from simple moral indignation to violent threats and outright hate speech:

> "This makes me very, very stabby...die off...move to a big fucking island somewhere and leave us...alone!!!!...people like you should just spontaneously combust for the sake of our society...you should be eradicated...you should be like, beaten up and raped...seriously go kill yourself."

Kindly note that all those unhinged and morally totalitarian quotes were from gay-rights *supporters*, not gay-bashers.

The sequence of events at Harps Marketplace way up in the Arkansas Ozarks went roughly like this: The magazine featuring the gay duo and their possibly gay baby was put on the racks. According to store management, "several" customers complained about it. The manager, following standard protocol when customers complain, decided to put up what is known as a "Family Shield" covering most of the magazine in order to "protect young Harps shoppers."

It was the Family Shield—not the in-your-face-and-down-your-throat gayness—that "shocked" and "horrified" local woman Jennifer Huddleston, who, at the risk of stereotyping, looks like she owns a lot of cats.

The gay-friendly Huddleston decided to get TWICE as offended as the anonymous local homophobes. She hopped onto Twitter beseeching the help of the ACLU, GLAAD, Anderson Cooper, Ellen DeGeneres, the shrieking orange cunt-monster Kathy Griffin, and the rest of the gay-friendly digital world, which came out in force to prove that they were far more technologically efficient at getting offended than a smattering of fundamentalist queer-baiters in the Arkansas hills.

It was during this furious and well-orchestrated backlash that we got a glimpse at how truly tolerant and accepting the gay coastal urban blogosphere is toward those whom they perceive as fundamentally "different" from them:

Bible thumping inbreds...bible beating mouth breathers...fuckin rednecks....They can't live in a world where people are different...its fucking ignorant white trash hicks like you that make this country so fucked up...white trash baby mommas with no baby daddy in sight who live on Hi-C and Doritos, smoke no-name brand cigarettes and scream at their kids 24/7....The SCARIEST part is that these midwestern YOKELS have the same voting rights we do. There must be so much METH in the air they breath [sic]...uneducated, idiotic, hate-mongering, ignorant...backwards ass hillbilly fuckholes....truly dumbfuck, missing tooth people....They would give their only tooth to fuck Elton....Yes the south is the butt of so many jokes because they have all taken one dip too many in the same gene pool.

The story was picked up by ABC, NBC, and CNN. It soon found its way into the UK's *Daily Mail*, the *India Times*, and the *Sydney Morning Herald*. The international press made blanket headline statements about how the magazine was "Censored In US" or "Censored in Arkansas," as if what happened was more far-reaching and culture-damning than a single incident at a single store in a single small American town.

Within a day, Harps executives relented to media pressure, removed the Family Shield, and issued a groveling apology about how "our employees and our customers come in all shapes and sizes, beliefs and preferences....Harps has never and would never discriminate." With triumphalist jubilation, major media declared that one brave girl had "shamed" a backwoods grocery store into removing the odious Hate Shield.

I remember back when public shaming was largely aimed *at* the homos. Nowadays it's the homos and their sob sisters who are eagerly doing most of the "outing" and public shaming. Either way, I'll pass.

After decades of insisting that the government get out of their bedrooms, gay activists are now insisting on their natural-born right, even if they have to hop in bed with the government to accomplish it, to drag their cum-spackled waterbeds straight into small grocery stores in rural areas where the majority of people might not want their four-year-olds to see it.

Not that anyone asked, but I preferred gay males when they were cultural outsiders who seemed impossible to offend. Nowadays they scream for mainstream acceptance and get offended at everything. Tsk-tsk, ladies! As outsiders, they used to see clearly through the idiocy of mass-culture moral panics. Now, as they squiggle and squirm to be accepted as "normal" rather than "different," they fabricate their own humorless moral panics. Frankly, the fags have disappointed me. If they keep up this pace, it will soon be impossible to distinguish them from the lesbians.

As I entered puberty, Elton John was unquestionably the world's hugest pop star—as big as Elvis in the 50s, The Beatles in the 60s, and Michael Jackson in the 80s. In the early to mid-70s, Elton's popularity rocketed deep into outer space while no one else so much as dented the clouds. Even The Beatles never had an album that entered the charts at #1, much less two albums in a row. The moment that *Captain Fantastic* was released, my ostensibly homophobic douchebag Italo-Catholic working-class next-door neighbors snapped it up and had it spinning on their turntable.

With his giant spangled boots and rhinestone glasses and peacock feathers and undeniably fey mannerisms, we all assumed that Elton John was, in the local argot, a "gaybird." It mattered not that he sang about "holdin' hands and skimmin' stones" with a girl named Suzie or how he begged Kiki Dee not to go breakin' his heart—it was a foregone conclusion that he was a born fairy.

And none of us cared that he was fruitier than Carmen Miranda's headpiece. That wasn't the issue. We liked his music. His flamboyance (code for "gayness") probably made him all the more exotically entertaining to us.

Although way back in the 1950s the USA was supposedly buried up to its asshole in homophobia, that didn't prevent Liberace from becoming the world's highest-paid entertainer all the way through to the 1970s. And if you couldn't tell that Liberace was gay, you shouldn't even be entitled to a driver's license.

Likewise, Elton John's unabashed Mummer's Parade level of, ehh, "theatricality" didn't stop Americans from embracing him openly in the 1970s...until the fateful 1976 *Rolling Stone* interview where he for the first time admitted he was, at the very least, bisexual. (It wasn't until a failed marriage to a German woman many years later that Elton finally conceded he was "comfortable" being all-gay, all the time.)

After Elton outed himself, his popularity in America instantly and palpably weakened. It seemed as if people had no problem *knowing* he was gay, but they got skeeved the moment it became an *issue*. It's the familiar complaint of "Don't shove your long, hard, throbbing, veiny, juicy agenda down our throats."

I find the magazine cover of Elton and David posing as if they were Ozzie and Harriet Nelson with their little pink designer-handbag infant to be even more distasteful and disturbing than when Elton was dressing up as Donald Duck. It seemed normal for Elton to be weird; what seems so weird are his half-cocked and possibly senile attempts to be normal.

There was nothing normal about their son's birth. Elton and David, with the scientific aid of the Center for Surrogate Parenting in Encino, CA, claim they mixed their semen together, which was then injected into Woman #1's vagina. Once one of their sperm fertilized Woman #1's egg, it was surgically removed and then planted into Woman #2's vagina. Neither woman's identity has been revealed, as they were presumably paid handsomely to keep quiet. And it's safe to assume that little Zachary Jackson Levon Furnish-John's inevitable quest for identity will be anything but normal.

To date, Elton John has not publicly commented on the Arkansas magazine-shielding scandal, but otherwise he can't keep his mouth shut about how he continues to suffer for being a homosexual. Despite his massive wealth, undoubted legions of paid minions, and widespread reputation as a tantrum-throwing diva, Elton recently wailed that he's "fed-up" with being treated like a "second-class citizen" in America.

For once in your life, Elton, quit acting like such a fag and show some taste and restraint. I've crunched the numbers. Your estimated net worth is more than the yearly income of every resident of Mountain Home, Arkansas combined. Let's be clear about who the "second-class citizens" are in this equation, OK, luvvie? Let's be honest about whose back the major media is protecting, m'kay? I don't see any of these Ozark hillbillies barging into the Castro District and demanding that everyone wave Rebel flags. So let them have their own culture. Obviously, Arkansas ain't the kind of place to raise your kid. In fact (in the winter at least), it's cold as hell. You've quit those days and your redneck ways, so better let the honky cats get back to the woods, darling. Isn't that what diversity and tolerance are all about?

Sir Elton John—if I may call you that—you have most of the rest of the world in which to mince freely as if you were Julie Andrews in *The Sound of Music*. So be a good sport and let them have the Ozarks. Have you ever even *been* to the Ozarks? Why has your insatiable lust for *Lebensraum* expanded so greatly that you suddenly need to flap your angel wings in the Ozarks, too? Give the Ozarks back to the Ozarkers and quit trying to pass for normal. Or do I have to shove you back in the closet before you start making good music again?

14

White Man Lectures White Girls About Calling Him A "Nigga"

On xoJane, one the world's premier comedy websites, a white man named David Alm wrote a very sensitive—one might even go so far as to call it "painful"—essay about a shocking incident he claims to have suffered on the New York subway.

He identifies himself as "a 38-year-old white man" who "fled my nearly all-white college town in southern Minnesota in 1998" and then went on to prove what a decent, noble, righteous human being he was not only to live among Puerto Ricans, Jews, blacks, and northern African Muslims, but to have lived for six years with a black woman and spawned actual, real-life, glow-in-the-dark black children with her. This guy really goes way the fuck out of his way to stand on a little white soapbox and prove he's not a racist in the best way known to humankind—by doing NOTHING but constantly talking about race.

In the name of the ever-lovin' bleedin' nonwhite Jesus Christ, this cat sounds like the most tolerant—and FUN—white man in the process of fleeing his whiteness in the whole wide world! The essay even boasts a photo of him with his black mating partner, whom it is presumed no longer mates with him since he keeps referring to her in the past tense.

He relates a story of how he was riding the F train to Manhattan, when what should happen but a pair of white girls shrieked at the sight of some black male friends, whereupon he "scowled" because he "couldn't help it." Although he doesn't exactly make it clear, I'm guessing he scowled at the shrieking, not the white girl/black guy scenario, because he also can't help explaining how he's not a racist.

After he scowls at them, one of the girls says to the other, "That nigga just glared at you." When her friend asks for clarification, she points at him and calls him a "bald-headed nigga," whereupon they both start laughing like pale-skinned hyenas at him.

He says "I knew I should ignore them," but as he's already made clear, he's the type of guy who just can't help himself. He walks up to them and coldly instructs them not to call him a "nigga." When they remain defiant to the bald-headed nigga, he launches into a pious tirade about oppression, history, slavery, hatred, and all the other shit that continues to underline the quite obvious fact that he is one happy-go-lucky nigga.

Then his essay launches into a boring litany about all the familiar hate-crime porn such as Rodney King and Amadou Diallo and how blacks are permitted to reclaim the word "nigga" but it still shouldn't be used by white men who breed with black women and teenage white girls who shriek at the sight of black males. He says that "there is something noble in my anger," even as the "nigga"-spewing white girls and their black male friends are laughing their asses off at him.

White nigga, pleez! The entire scenario is possibly the most hilarious thing I've heard all year—white man flees white people to live and breed among black people, and yet white and black people alike treat him like the self-righteous nerd he is when he tries lecturing them about racism.

This story gives me more hope for the future of American race relations than anything I've heard in years.

15

The Other "N" Word

Embroiled in a high-profile standoff with the feds over taxes and land rights in the spring of 2014, Nevada rancher Cliven Bundy dropped an "N" bomb on camera.

The cattle-ropin', cowboy-hat-wearin', tax-protestin' Mr. Bundy made reference to "the Negro" in the same way one mentions Bigfoot, the Abominable Snowman, or "the white man"—as if there were only one Negro rather than many:

I want to tell you one more thing I know about the Negro....They abort their young children, they put their young men in jail, because they never learned how to pick cotton. And I've often wondered, are they better off as slaves, picking cotton and having a family life and doing things, or are they better off under government subsidy?

For reasons you will probably never understand, I find that entire quote funny. What's even funnier is that much of the predictable Twit-rage and Face-palming focused on the mere fact that he dared to use the word "Negro." Forget about the Alzheimer's level of confusion in the rest of the quote.

During last Saturday's soliloquy, Bundy also referred to "colored people"—we all know the preferred term is "people of color"—and "the Mexicans" in some meandering statements about slavery, the Watts Riots, and government dependency. Here's the clip. Nevada looks so dry, I get thirsty just watching this:

OK, so when did "Negro" become a dirty word?

Granted, it's not considered as unspeakably obscene as the other "N" word—you know, the one that rhymes with bigger, chigger, ditch-digger, jigger, Tigger, and wigger—but this polite-sounding word has been banned from polite company for reasons that elude me.

I realize you're not *supposed* to say it; I don't understand *why*. It's the Spanish word for "black." Why is that an outrage? We are currently encouraged to call American persons of African ancestry "black," but it's racist to call them the Spanish word for "black"? If anything, banning the word "Negro" is disrespectful to Spaniards. What about *their* rights? Hmm?

I think it's a very happy-sounding word, and any negative connotations it has acquired over the years are due not only to hypersensitivity, but also possibly to hypertension as a result of the high fat and sodium content found in many fried foods. Say it out loud to yourself while standing in front of a mirror and try not to smile. It's almost like when a photographer tells you to say "cheese"—it's hard not to grin when saying "Negro." Don't be afraid of the word—it's friendlier than you'd think. *Nee-grow. Nee-grow.* See? It has a lilting, lyrical quality all its own.

It was a commonly used and perfectly benign-sounding word back when I was going to grade school with your grandfather. I don't *ever* remember it being used disrespectfully. Back then I pictured your average "Negro" as having very nice teeth, a proper set of eyeglasses, and perhaps even a collegiate sweater. I remember seeing Negroes on the TV. I remember liking them, too.

"Negro" is a good word that has been given an unfairly bad

reputation by those with bad motivations, so I call for its complete and utter rehabilitation.

16

The Importance Of Gender-Neutral Public Restrooms For Bisexual Space Aliens

We've all been repeatedly told that gender is only a "social construct."

We are also asked to believe that this particular social construct just so happened—*what are the chances?*—to have been artificially constructed almost *precisely* the same way across the globe in every culture throughout history. All those penises and vaginas—you know, not only the ones on male and female humans, but also on barnyard animals as well as the filthy and lascivious insects that prey upon their furry hides—are merely visual phantasms conjured from the fraudulent meanings that privileged patriarchal capitalistic corporate-sponsored heteronormative societies foist upon oppressed peoples.

Or something. There seems to be no end to the inane, reality-defying mantras of modern progressive education, mantras that seek to build and sustain—through force if necessary—a world that makes absolutely no sense.

It can't possibly be that those pesky and elusive "social constructs" are often derived from biological realities, and this artificial thing called "gender" has some basis in those palpable things called "genitals."

While we're at it, I should remind you that race isn't real, although racism is.

And rape is all about power and has nothing to do with sex, despite, again, the persistence of all those penises and vaginas.

Right. And I have some upside-down urinals I'd like to sell you.

By the way—I *like* urinals. I've always liked them. It may be going a little too far to say I "enjoy" them, but, yes, I like them. I like going into a public restroom and knowing they have contraptions that allow me to void my bladder without sitting on a sticky ocean of germs and waste material. I savor the fact that if I've had one too many coffees, I can dash into a public men's room and drain the main vein without having to sit. I realize that women can't do this, but that's what nature intended. I'm OK with all that.

And yet there are those—mostly young, mostly naïve, mostly gay, mostly devoid of rudimentary reasoning skills—who deign to come and take away my urinals in their mad quest to make everything "gender-neutral" so the ridiculously tiny minority of genuine biological hermaphrodites can live their lives not feeling quite so uncomfortable as they otherwise would in situations requiring them to either urinate or defecate in public places.

Most disturbingly, the people who push this nonsense are clustered most stubbornly in our places of higher education.

I graduated from college in the mid-80s, and even then nearly all my teachers, especially in journalism, were self-admitted communists or at least "sympathizers." In the intervening years, I'd had a vague sense that American education had drifted ever more slowly and stubbornly toward the rancid and insatiable pieties of cultural Marxism.

This became all too real for me the day when my son, only three years old and attending some kind of pre-pre-preschool, received a homework assignment where he had to honor his favorite figure in black history. (We made him do DJ Kool Herc just to confuse the teachers.)

But mind you, they were requiring that he honor black idols *before they started teaching him to read and write*. There's something very, very wrong there. You might even say they have it all ass-backwards.

Through careful examination of leaked documents and rigorous interviews with confidential informants, I have recently fallen under the impression that the School of the Art Institute of Chicago (SAIC) is a place where parents blow about $40K a year so their kids can go dumpster-diving for rotted vegetables, play bongos late at night, and distribute free bagels to the homeless, with whom they often have unprotected sex.

From all appearances, it's a place where the liberal-arts curriculum consists of teaching art students to be liberals, where the scourge of critical theory has entirely displaced critical thinking. It's also a place where young and freewheeling spirits tell one another to check their privilege and to always use appropriate pronouns that sensitively reflect one another's self-designated gender identity. You wouldn't want to "misgender" someone, after all.

It's a soft, warm, emotionally nurturing place where you can take both English and Art classes on Marx, although I'm not sure how he's relevant to either discipline. You can also take classes called "Class Warfare," "The Cuban Revolution," and "Climate Change: Locally/Globally." If you're feeling especially edgy, there are also classes called "Getting Weird & Hilarious" and "Art of Crossing the Street."

But if you want to go just bonkers with the postmodern deconstructive gender-bending Queer Theory anti-educational full-blown indoctrination stuff, Tuesdays at SAIC prove that the long prance through the institutions is complete.

That's where you can spend your entire afternoon and early evening grinding through a pair of three-hour courses called "Sci-Fi Queered" and "Gendered and Sexed-up Spaces."

From the syllabus to "Sci-Fi Queered":

This course takes as its archive a wave of feminist and queer science fiction written in the late twentieth century. The selected texts each have their own way of embedding gender construction in new and/or futuristic technologies, and we will be scrutinizing the imbrication of utopian possibilities for queered gender with the products of corporate control and asking where threads of dystopia and utopia may actually align.

Coinciding with a wave of feminism in America, our texts have each taken as their building blocks for new possibilities of gender the very stereotypes, caricatures, and dehumanizing structures of subjectivity forced on them by dominant cultures.

Wow. And they can cover all that in a single semester? Required reading for the course includes *The Female Man*, *Technologies of the Gendered Body*, and *He, She, and It*.

By the way—that course is taught by a woman, so I guess you know what *that* means.

From the syllabus to "Gendered and Sexed-up Spaces":

Situated at the intersection of queer and architectural theories, this course examines the pivotal role architecture and design play in the construction and performance of gender and sexuality. From public restrooms to gay bathhouses, gym locker rooms to sacred spaces, brothels to the suburban tract house, the built environment is a collection of conscious efforts to regulate, segregate, and create order among the sexes, genders, and sexualities based on heteronormative assumptions concerning body and mind.

Whew! You got all that? The required-reading list includes these doozies: "Finding a Place to Go: The Transgender Bathroom Dilemma," "Restriction and Reclamation: Lesbian Bars and Beaches of the 1950s," "Whoring in Utopia," "The History of Gay Bathhouses," and "Spontaneous pleasures: Sex between women in public places."

By the way—that course is taught by a man, so I guess you know what *that* means.

Well, in the event that we're someday faced with a dilemma where queer space aliens who are visiting our planet need to find a public restroom where they don't feel their precious sexuality and gender identity are being unfairly ignored or maligned, I suppose that some of this information could be useful in a real-world setting.

Otherwise, I'm not seeing any educational value here.

And they wonder why the US education system is fucked. Please spear this monster in the heart. It's gone too far. Teach the kids how to read, write, and use the Internet. After that, let their curiosity lead the way. Teach them how to use the tools, and if they're halfway smart, they can figure out the rest. But don't teach them what to *think*. It's tacky.

This school's list of courses sounds so fundamentally hostile to heterosexual males, I wouldn't be surprised if you had to spit on a severed penis that they keep in a velvet box before they hand you your diploma.

I'm warning you—you can have my urinal when you pry it from my cold, dead...OK, let's leave it at that.

17

It's Hard Out Here For A Dudebro

When I was a kid, a "dude" was a cowboy who worked on a ranch and had an abiding fondness for his horse. I didn't start hearing "dude" used as a generic term meaning "dumb, hairy, cloddish male" until the late 1970s, when suddenly my world seemed flooded with dudes.

In decades gone by, "bro" was a term of endearment almost exclusively used among black males, who later famously abandoned it *en masse* in favor of "homie."

Now cometh the "dudebro," an obnoxious term used to describe an obnoxious type of individual. My task here today is to determine who's more obnoxious: those who use the word as a slur, or the dudebros themselves.

Although the pejorative "dudebro" may be new to you, you've seen the type. And it *is* a sociological type—perhaps even a genetic one. I'm not sure what causes it, although I'd reckon there's some correlation with high testosterone and low intelligence. In terms of cognitive capacity, the dudebro is the peer of the female bimbo—in other words, dumb as a cheese doodle.

Mike "The Situation" Sorrentino from *Jersey Shore* is an archetypal East Coast dudebro, while chubby peroxided idiot celebrity chef Guy Fieri represents the West Coast strain. David Puddy, Elaine's meatheaded boyfriend on *Seinfeld*, is perhaps the most perfectly rendered dudebro in comedic history.

In previous incarnations such types have been known as "douchebags," "douches," "jocks," "frat boys," and "male chauvinist pigs." For decades now they have been more benignly known simply as "dudes," yet the newer term "dudebro" is heavily salted with sneering progressive condescension.

In this sense "dudebro" is like earlier pejoratives such as "yuppie" and "hipster"—hardly anyone uses such terms as a self-descriptor. Instead, it's nearly always used to demean someone *else*. And just as the term "racist" has come to mean "any white person who's OK with being white," the word "dudebro" is an ever-expanding catchall term to describe any male who's OK with being male. It is a testosterone-aversive gendered slur intended to induce shame in one's very male essence, to evoke repulsion at the very thought of one's precious male bodily fluids.

The term "dudebro" allegedly first appeared in the online gaming community to describe players with an affinity for macho, eminently dudely games such as *Madden* and *Call of Duty*. The social-justice community later adopted it to describe any male who shows warning signs of possessing testosterone.

The dudebro is severely masculine, often cartoonishly so, and frequently exaggerates his physical and sexual prowess through elaborate and ongoing rituals of compensation. He guzzles protein shakes and measures his penis daily. He's comically horny yet doesn't have the first clue about how to seduce a woman. He emits an aroma that is a disconcerting mélange of hotel disinfectant and baloney sandwiches. He shows no outward respect for bitches or fags, although he and his dudebro friends are constantly calling *one another* bitches and fags. He is likely to have a tribal tattoo, or at least one in Asian lettering that he doesn't understand. He practices mixed martial arts in his backyard and likes to fancy himself as "extreme." He may, at any given time, suddenly appear in flip-flops wearing cargo shorts, a puka-shell necklace, and a Hawaiian shirt while pumping his fist and going "WOO-HOO!" He typically likes to drink himself insensate and would not be the least ashamed to appear in public wearing one of those hats that holds your beer can and enables you to sip your favorite malt beverage through a straw. He prefers to drive a truck even though he doesn't need one. There's a good chance he's tried steroids.

Oh—and he's white. Black and Hispanic males who exhibit similarly idiotic levels of machismo are exempted from the cultural stigma that afflicts the lonely white dudebro.

In a plotline that reads something akin to *The Protocols of the Privileged Dudebros of Silicon Valley*, social-justice warriors have been sounding alarums that the tech industry is a festering haven of unabashed spermy maleness, with all the moral and literal stench that such a thing entails. In 2013 a mulatto female caused a huge stink by overreacting to a benign joke she'd heard from some male tech geeks sitting behind her at a conference. Then came tech-world honcho Pax Dickinson's firing as the result of a Tweet that used the word "boobies." Salon tells us that Dickinson's ritual expulsion "is just one example of how *dudebro* culture has powered—and stunted—the tech industry for the past decade." Man-hating pseudo-male PZ Myers claims the tech industry foments "a culture of self-congratulatory dudebros."

Their solution is preposterously simple: Flood the tech industry with whiny women and beta males who possess a strident, militant, all-consuming hatred for dudebros.

This rabid, unhinged bigotry toward dudebros is so intense in some corners that people encourage violence, more violence, and even yet more violence against them.

Hapless and uncomprehending dudebros are expected to passively sit with their hands folded in their laps as they're scolded over their cisgendered privilege and the fact that they deny the "brovantages" that life under this white-male patriarchy has granted them. They are told to shut the fuck up and stop pretending to listen, that they are in effect the brownshirts of rape culture for whom no form of surgical castration could be too painful.

If there's one personality trait that defines social activists, it is a bitterness that never dies. That's why I try my best to avoid them. I'd rather have someone high-five me than wag a finger at me.

I once spent an evening near Christmas with about a half-dozen Midwestern dudebros at a small home in a snowy Chicago suburb. They were friends of a pal of mine in his mid-40s who took me to meet these jovial douchebags he'd known since Catholic high school. The host was a part-time amateur hockey player who looked exactly like Fred Flintstone with a missing tooth. A giant bulldog of a dudebro who was having marital problems cooked some hearty tender beef strips while reminiscing about doing acid in college. The assembled dudebros insufflated copious amounts of cocaine and crushed one empty beer can after the next. I know this sounds like I'm making it up, but they actually passed around a copy of *Juggs* magazine. At around 2AM they all decided we should go to some weird sorta-strip club where girls spin around on brass poles in lingerie without taking off a stitch of clothing and yet still try to hit you up for tips.

How much hate would I need to have in my heart not to love those guys? In six hours, I didn't hear the term "white privilege" once, nor did I hear anyone complain that the strip club wasn't diverse enough. Contrary to the social-justice crowd's delusions, nobody said they wanted to rape anyone—not even *once*. So I can forgive the dudebros their fundamental and incurable tackiness because they were all friendly and not the least bit self-righteous. There are greater crimes than being cheesy—like, for example, being insufferable.

Dudebros, I've got your back in this war.

18

From Red Scare To Rainbow Scare

Brendan Eich, the creator of JavaScript, was forced to resign in 2014 as CEO of Mozilla as a result of pressure from gay-rights activists. Eich had lasted only a little longer than a week as Mozilla's CEO.

What led to his swift demise was the fact that in 2008, Eich had donated $1,000 to support California's Proposition 8, a bill that simply stated:

> *Only marriage between a man and a woman is valid or recognized in California.*

Doesn't anyone remember that in the same year, Barack Obama also opposed gay marriage?

Despite all the propaganda you hear about how mountains of right-wing money supposedly corrupt the electoral process, gay-marriage supporters donated $44,123,811 to stop Proposition 8—an advantage of more than $5 million compared to campaign contributors who supported "traditional marriage." Despite that, California voters didn't listen to the money and favored Proposition 8 by a margin of 52% to 48%. This is an essential flaw of democracy, and one that doesn't get nearly enough attention—if voters are outnumbered by a slim margin of 4%, the losing 48% walk away with *nothing*.

Still, it took only one US District Judge to overturn what seven million voters wanted. So on top of sloppy democracy, you have a dictatorial judiciary, and only boobs and rubes think that judges are unbiased.

I belong to a small and largely voiceless minority who believe that the state shouldn't have *any* role in sanctioning marriage, gay or straight. And I'm amused that gays are pushing so hard for it, because if they'd ever actually *been* married, they might not be so enthusiastic about the whole project.

As I will continually remind you before you get a chance to remind me, I am much older than most of you, which I feel gives me a wider perspective on recent events. The fact that I was born before you was not a matter of choice—like skin color and, as many of you insist, sexual orientation—so I'd suggest you pipe down with the "ageism" before I curl myself in a ball and start crying in the shower again.

What I've witnessed over the years is a seismic shift in societal intolerance, especially in what it means to be a "liberal." When I was a kid, the censors and book-burners and witch-hunters were exclusively right-wingers. They were the ones who sought to get you fired for thinking or behaving differently, especially if they thought you were a communist or gay or supported interracial sex.

And there seemed to be a stretch of time—roughly between 1970 and 1990—when the right-wing witch-hunters were largely shouted down. I'm sure that others' experiences may be different, but during that golden little sliver of time, I don't remember many people getting fired and boycotted and run out of town for thinking or behaving differently. It was truly the closest I've ever seen the USA come to resembling a tolerant society.

But by the early 1990s, as the PC Panzer tanks had rolled into every university and every courtroom, the intolerance started coming more and more from the left.

In *The Daily Dish*, the openly gay Andrew Sullivan has called Eich's resignation "The Hounding Of A Heretic":

> *If this is the gay rights movement today – hounding our opponents with a fanaticism more like the religious right than anyone else – then count me out. If we are about intimidating the free speech of others, we are no better than the anti-gay bullies who came before us.*

I couldn't agree more with that diminutive bearded homo. These days, the government, the educational system, and the media—three huge pillars of power—generally fall in lockstep with the progressive narrative. Unlike the 1970s when I was an impressionable kid who absorbed my politics from Norman Lear TV sitcoms, modern society generally supports blacks and gays and women while gleefully shitting on the very *concept* of white men.

The problem is that increasingly these days, intolerance is aimed like gunfire at those who think differently. It doesn't matter that those who support the firing and branding and shaming of dissenters are convinced they're finally fighting for an unassailably moral cause—that's how *all* totalitarians think.

The Red Scare of my youth has now been supplanted by a Rainbow Scare. I believe that the term "rights" is a dubious concept—i.e., the government can't *give* rights, it can only *take* them—but the right to *think* differently should at least be as valuable as the right to engage in butt-sex without some mob of closeted jerkoffs clobbering you with baseball bats. America, you need to loosen your ideological sphincter and start tolerating disagreement, or we're headed straight—pun intended—into another Dark Age.

19

TV Star Loses 70 Pounds, Attacks His Fat Critics, And Gets His Food Show Pulled

I only know Adam Richman from watching a few episodes of his show *Man v. Food*, which featured him shoving buckets of lard-dripping food down his throat in portions big enough to burst a colon. Every episode had him trying to eat a hamburger the size of a truck wheel or a hoagie large enough to crawl inside and take a nap. It seemed inevitable that one day he would die from overeating, just as I suspect that Andrew "Bizarre Foods" Zimmern will one day eat something so weird that it kills him, and just as everyone suspected that Steve "Crocodile Hunter" Irwin would eventually tussle with an aquatic beast that murdered him.

Richman has toned down the gluttony, though, and shaved

70 pounds from his oleaginous frame, and the most immediately apparent cosmetic result is that he looks slightly more Jewish. He posed for a semi-nude photo in the British version of *Cosmpolitan* which is revolting—even though he isn't eating hoagies anymore, he still *looks* like one.

He has apparently been working on a new show—one less gladiatorial in its approach toward the gustatory arts—called *Man Finds Food* that was supposed to debut, but he went and blew it all to hell by posting what he is now, in hindsight, calling "inexcusable remarks" against a cabal of fat people for supposedly fat-shaming them by boasting that he lost so much weight.

He got the ball rolling—or, if you prefer, the flab undulating—by posting a slimmed-down picture of himself on Instagram.

Almost immediately he was accused of fat-shaming, of glorifying negative body images, and of triggering girls with eating disorders whose emotions go haywire when they see the hashtag #thinspiration.

A self-described "fat activist" who calls herself Amber Sarah and is roughly the size of Croatia claims that "thinspiration is very popular in pro-anorexia and pro-bulimia circles." Exactly what that means, I suppose we'll never know. She posted on Adam's Instagram page that the word "thinspiration" is "problematic"—apparently even more problematic than diabetes and heart disease.

The fat-no-more Richman then launched into a poo-flinging contest against a few metric tons of fat activists. He used the acronym "DILLIGAF?" (do I look like I give a fuck?) and told someone who calls themselves "the fattest fox" to "eat a bag of shit" and that the only "fuckup it seems [is] your Dad's choice to go without a condom." He told another "fatacceptance / bodypositivity" activist (fattivist?) to "grab a razor blade & draw a bath. I doubt anyone will miss you."

Then, realizing he'd lost his shit and may lose his show as a result, he pecked out a quick apology:

I've long struggled with my body image and have worked very hard to achieve a healthy weight. I'm incredibly sorry to everyone I've hurt.

Adam Richman may have plenty of extra time now to keep struggling with his body image, as the Travel Channel has postponed *Man Finds Food* indefinitely.

The moral of the story is that you should never bite the hand that feeds you hoagies.

20

Texas Cheerleader Poses For Photos With Animals She's Killed, Gets Death Threats

In the eyes of many, Kendall Jones's first sin is that she's from Texas. Compounding matters is the fact that she's a blonde teenage cheerleader. But what's chafing the flabby calves of the blogosphere's sundry animal-rights misfits is the fact that she's a big-game huntress who sees no shame in posing for pictures with the animals she's just killed and then sharing the photos online. In their minds, this makes her a bigoted redneck privileged animal-murdering cracker—one who must suffer and even be killed for her transgressions.

Naturally, the Full-Time Shamers online are doing everything in their power to shame her. And since she is perceived to be preying on "defenseless" mammals, they also see no irony or hypocrisy in openly wishing that she gets brutally murdered: "You're the pest – and need to be hunted down," wrote one guest on her Facebook page. "I hope you get stomped to death by an elephant," wrote another.

On Twitter, she's facing the same sort of fire-breathing hatred that has become *de rigueur* among those faceless flesh-blobs who cloak their hatred behind a shield of compassion:

> *Kendall Jones is a piece of crap. Feed her to the Lions*
> — Michael Shadow (@yborcityfl)

> *Kendall Jones, what a piece of shit*
> — Alexander Webster (@princezaet)

> *#KendallJones a horrible human. Try hunting your "lions and tigers and bears" without a gun, then let's see who the bloody cheerleader is.*
> — MeganMonreaux (@MeganMonreaux) July 1, 2014

> *Someone give Kendall Jones a pair of running shoes and hand me a rifle. We'll see how long she defends her 'fair chase' logic.*
> — Felice Fawn (@felicefawn)

What I'd like to see is for any of these perpetually outraged keyboard warriors to be dropped alone on the African plains with only their hands to defend themselves. Let's see how loving and equality-minded the lions and hippos and leopards are to them then.

This is, yet again, why the idea of equality is so dumb and ultimately destructive—it ignores the fact that nature is largely more predatory and conflict-ridden than it is harmonious. It took untold millennia of evolutionary trials and errors for humans to get to the point where they were able to kill lions rather than be eaten by them, and suddenly we're so soft and "evolved" that many of us see this as a matter of shame rather than of pride. This is a sign of a species in decline.

But the big giveaway—the thing that proves her critics are far more motivated by hostility than compassion—is the open blood-lust they fling at her. She is a threat to their herd mentality, so she must be shamed, stomped, eviscerated, and murdered. In their blind, dumb, rampaging self-righteousness, in their public-square chest-thumping quest to prove that they are somehow above other murderous humans, they ignore the fact that their unrealistically romanticized wild animals are also murderous. And the topper is that they reveal that deep down, they, too, are murderous animals. Every word they type shows blood dripping from their fangs. But they are simultaneously too dumb to see the contradiction and too cowardly to take matters into their own hands.

Personally, I love animals far more than I love people, which suggests a certain level of social maladjustment on my part. With rare exceptions, I'd rather spend time with a cat or a dog than with another human. But I've also run across people whose noses are buried so deep in animal waste, they can't see how it's warped their ability to interact with other humans on any meaningful level. I'm thinking in particular of a family member who at one point owned more than 90 cats simultaneously and who at last count owned 30 dogs and 20 cats, all of them stuffed into a tiny two-bedroom cottage. This person was pilled-up out of their head on near-lethal amounts of painkillers at any given time and didn't seem to care in the least how their daughter had just fatally overdosed alone on pills in a motel room and how their stepson had morphed into an HIV-positive crack whore who routinely robbed the family of all their belongings. But God forbid one of the household's numberless squirming canines came down with the sniffles—it was an immediate, all-consuming crisis.

This person also eagerly joined in all of the tiresome online petitions calling the for the heads of anyone suspected of animal abuse. I saw them express far more rage at the Michael Vick dog-torturing case than at the fact their daughter had died alone of an overdose. I witnessed them out of their mind with anger at a picture, possibly Photoshopped, of two grinning teen boys who'd just lynched a cat—far more anger than they showed whenever the HIV-positive crack-whore stepson would burglarize their house and strip it of everything worth more than $5.

So as much as I love animals, I've personally witnessed how anthropomorphizing them to the point where they have "rights" is often the domain of severely maladapted human beings—ones who suck both at being humans and at realizing they are also animals, with all of the selfish, predatory instincts such status implies.

In other words, it's fine if you want to save the whales, but I doubt the whales give a fuck about you.

21

Suey Park, You Are A Fucking Dingbat

Suey Park, the humorless desiccated vadge who launched the #CancelColbert Twitter campaign because she couldn't take a joke wherein a white man was joking about racist white men because "whiteness" dictates that all white men are racist, even the ones who are earnestly attempting to lampoon white racism—or *something*—is stretching out her fifteen minutes of fame to eighteen or maybe even eighteen and a half.

She did an interview published on Salon, that baby viper's nest of white ethno-masochism that nurtures and coddles and enables nonwhites to hate whites as much as the *extremely* white and *truly* privileged white staffers hate their own whiteness, all of this grotesque moralistic showboating nudged along by *über*-white staffers such as that hideous carved pumpkin Joan Walsh and that low-sodium weenie sandwich Alex Pareene.

Ms. Park describes herself as an "activist," which all working people realize is a person who isn't actively performing activities at an actual job. She also calls herself a "comedian," although she didn't say one fucking funny thing in the interview and as far as I know has never done one funny thing in her life—besides, perhaps, existing.

During the interview—which had one unintentionally funny moment because she was momentarily distracted by a bird outside her window and forgot what question she was answering—she confessed she hadn't seen Colbert's televised response to her campaign and rudely snapped at the interviewer (who, as Salon's benevolent tokenism would have it, was also a WOC) that it was "an irrelevant question" to ask whether she'd seen it.

She also dilated her mental vagina and squeezed out the following thought-queefs for all the world to see:

I think as a result of the white ally industrial complex, for too long people of color have been asked to censor whiteness, they have been asked to educate their oppressor, they have been asked to use the right tone, and appease their politics in order to be heard. And in an effort to just contribute to the self-improvement of white allies that are often times just racist.

LMFAO! ROFL! ROFL&LMFAO!!! You're *killin'* me, lady! Quick, Lorne Michaels—get this chick a spot on the newer, more diverse *SNL*!

She also said:

I'm talking about whiteness at large.

You want to talk about whiteness at large? OK, then so do I—according to this, white penises are much larger than Korean ones, which supposedly average a highly comedic 3.8 inches.

Suey—which, last I checked, was what pig farmers shouted when calling their hogs—also insinuated it was wrong to want to "humanize the oppressor," which I'm assuming she means whites and their unforgivably white whiteness. And truly, I can't imagine the burden of oppression that Asians bear in this stinkingly racist white society. Oh, to suffer an average family income over $12,000 more than white families! Oh, to have an average life expectancy of 7.6 years longer than your evil white oppressors! Oh, the horror that Asian Americans hold bachelor's degrees at a rate roughly 20% higher than the US population as a whole! The pain! The agony! The oppression! Quick—somebody grab me a box of Kleenex, so long as they aren't white!

I always paint my white characters to be singular, to be ignorant....

Nope, nothin' racist about that, because, as we all know, whites suffer unfair privileges, even though, as already noted, Asians in America live longer and make more money than whites. We're talking about "structural" racism, "invisible" racism—you know, the kind you can never quantify because it doesn't really exist.

When asked what was the best way to work with America's humbly supine and eternally apologetic white population, she said:

I don't want them on our side...This is not reform, this is revolution....Whiteness will always be the enemy.

It's *revolting*, but it's not a revolution. It's not even a bowel movement. And you seem to want a "war" where your "enemy" has already surrendered, or at least is required to fight with his mouth taped shut and his hands tied behind his back.

The light bulb over her head burns so dimly that she can't even tell the difference between "critical thinking" and warmed-over Frankfurt School critical theory. The first makes no presumptions, while the second starts with the premise "Western Civilization is evil" and tries to cram the facts into fit the pseudo-religious Guilt Narrative. With critical thinking, all facts are weighed objectively; with critical theory, inconvenient facts are dismissed as thoughtcrimes.

[T]his is a problem with white supremacy that it's still nonviolent and it's still violent and it's still violent violent....

Huh? What? I'm sorry—come again? I got distracted. An Asian dingbat just flew past my window.

22

Is It A Hate Crime
To Make Fun Of
Short People?

(FULL DISCLOSURE AND TRIGGER WARNING: Do not read this if you are sent into an emotional tailspin by discussions of innate evolutionary height disparities among human beings. The author of this article is 5'11", which places him only slightly above the average for Americans of his gender and race. On average, white American males are slightly taller than black American males, and both groups are taller than Mexican-American males, although you probably already knew that, at least about the Mexicans. On average, all three groups of males are taller than females of any race for reasons which are undoubtedly caused by intersectional issues of oppression, nutrition, capitalism, colonialism, white privilege, and patriarchy. Monsanto is also probably largely to blame. As we all know, any measurable disparity between human groups is strictly the result of social forces rather than biological ones, and if you disagree, we will start a Change.org petition to have you fired from your job, you fucking hateful asshole subhuman piece of shit.)

In our ongoing quest to annihilate oppression and unfairness wherever we imagine it to be, have we perhaps been shortsighted? Have we neglected one perennially mocked group simply because they may have flown in under our radar? Is this a case where we can't see the forest because of the shrubs?

Heightism is real. Or at least it's a real word coined in 1971 by sociologist Saul Feldman, who at press time was unavailable to be measured. He delivered a paper with the unwieldy title of "The presentation of shortness in everyday life—height and heightism in American society: Toward a sociology of stature" to the American Psychological Association, and it's not known whether he had to stand on a stack of telephone books to deliver his speech. (Back then, interestingly enough, the average American male was two inches shorter than he is now, so although we appear to be making progress, we need to address the race and gender gaps before we can even pretend to have achieved Height Justice in the USA.)

Pint-sized British politician John Bercow, who may be able to do the limbo rock standing up since he measures a diminutive 5'6", recently likened criticism of the vertically challenged to racism and homophobia:

> *Whereas nobody these days would regard it as acceptable to criticise someone on grounds of race or creed or disability or sexual orientation, somehow it seems to be acceptable to comment on someone's height, or lack of it.*

Bercow has repeatedly been mocked by political opponents for his height deficiencies, at one point being smeared as a "stupid, sanctimonious dwarf." Although he claims he was "never bothered about being short," methinks the pocket-sized pol doth protest too much.

Some studies claim that on average, a man's wages increase for every additional inch in his height. Yet this tragic "wage gap" gets roughly the same amount of attention as a 5'3" male standing alone in a ballroom with no one willing to be his dance partner. Isn't it time we also called out the phrase "tall, dark, and handsome" as being innately discriminatory toward short, ugly white guys?

An article from ABC News quotes a 5'4" lonely Ohioan named Jeff who bemoans the fact that if he were fat he could exercise and diet, while if he were ugly, he could rely on plastic surgery to reverse the savagery that nature had visited upon his visage. But since he is short, there is currently no surgical resource for what is essentially a disability of attractiveness.

That may be sad—at least if you're short—but it's also true. I'm reminded of a joke that Catskills comic Freddie Roman once told at the expense of *Seinfeld*'s Jason Alexander (who is 5'5") at a roast. It went something along the lines of, "Mr. Alexander, you are living proof that all of the wealth, power, and fame in the world cannot buy height."

For now, we can only hope and pray that science will soon find a cure for the small fry among us. Keep hope alive, short people—there's a light at the top of the tunnel.

23

Criticizing PC Totalitarianism—A "90s Thing"?

I've noticed a meme spreading among beardo progressive types—who seem especially vulnerable to swallowing dumb memes so long as it helps them feel warm 'n' snugly cocooned within their ideological ingroup—to reduce any criticism of PC totalitarianism as a "90s thing."

Obviously we're dealing with pop-culture inbreds whose thinking is so superficial, they view even political debates as fashion trends. "Dude, criticizing PC witch hunts went out of style around the time Bob Mould went solo."

I must have missed the report that came out in 2000 that irrefutably proved blank-slate human equality. And I must be imagining that the American media, which is funded in large part by globalist oligarchs, is screaming daily about racism and homophobia and "white males" with more shrillness than they even did in the 90s.

I keep challenging progressives to debates because I'm confident their thinking is shallow and emotion-based rather than a logical belief system. There is no proof of human equality, either among individuals or groups, yet they shriek like clubbed seals when you dare challenge their most sacred pseudo-religious notions. This is why it'd be fun to debate them in a moderated forum where the debate could be recorded for posterity—I'm confident I could easily peel through their flimsy notions of culture, race, and equality and unmask them for the sloppy thinkers they are.

I've noticed that progressives—who talk mighty shit and then run, because they're ill-equipped to really deal with any challenges to their holiest precepts—never seem capable or willing to actually debate their fundamental beliefs. I've concluded it's because deep down, they're not entirely secure with their beliefs. Their beliefs are the result of New Agey wishful thinking rather than logic. This is why they must declare certain topics to be forever settled and beyond debate. Because, let's face it, the idea of "equality" withers and dies under the merest scrutiny. Such are the delusions of "liberal creationism," which posits that evolution is real, yet it somehow magically stopped the moment all the world's diverse social groups arrived at the finish line simultaneously.

Modern PC witch-hunting is far worse than McCarthyism, which is why it needs to be addressed, challenged, and smothered with logic wherever it appears.

Why is it worse than McCarthyism? How *dare* I equate the two, much less allege that what's going on now is worse?

Because in the 1950s, communists were actually killing people in the millions. Mao's Great Leap Forward took tens of millions of lives in the late 1950s. People were being worked and starved to death in Soviet gulags. Political dissidents in communist countries were sent to prison or mental hospitals. Imagine that—a political belief system founded on the notion of human equality resorted to totalitarian tactics in order to maintain itself. Of *course* it did! That's the only way to maintain a fraudulent belief system—by silencing all dissent.

These days, actual racially motivated white-on-black violence is so rare, the witch-hunters have to pretend an obviously Hispanic guy named George Zimmerman magically becomes "white" merely to maintain their hopelessly outdated narrative. They also have to turn a blind eye to black mob attacks on whites in order to keep reminding everyone about 100-year-old lynchings. If I'm stuck in the 90s, why do you keep talking about racially motivated violence that happened 100 years ago while I keep talking about incidents that happened this week? Who's truly stuck in the past here?

PC witch-hunting is also similar to McCarthyism in that people are losing their jobs and facing group ridicule and ostracism merely for *thinking* differently. In 1950s America, if you diverted from the herd's beliefs about capitalism, you were a pariah. Same goes today if you dare question modern orthodoxies about race. So it's a mortal sin to not tolerate different skin colors but somehow righteous to be stubbornly intolerant of all ideological dissent? Is trying to destroy someone's life because they *think* differently somehow better than not hiring them for being gay or black? If so, I'm not seeing it. I believe in freedom of association and that people should be able to hire (or refuse to hire) whomever they want. But growing up Catholic—and leaving it once I peered through its illogic, just as I fled liberalism so many years ago—I formed a strong distaste for moralistic witch hunts. All this screeching about "racism" is always framed in moralistic rather than logical terms. Hence, you have people who say "race doesn't exist," but somehow they magically see "racism" everywhere, yet they're blind to how hopelessly contradictory such propositions are.

Of *course* the liberal witch-hunters emulate McCarthyism, with one huge difference—communism was stacking up far more bodies in the 1950s than "racism" is today.

24

The Shame Sham

Like all societies before it, our society considers nothing more shameful than to be shameless. Thus, the Internet—which binds our society together like cheese binds a colon—is crammed with so much public shaming, it should be ashamed of itself.

Sticking your fist into the electronic beehive, you will be bitten by a thousand types of public shaming: age-shaming v. youth-shaming, slut-shaming v. virgin-shaming, fat-shaming v. skinny-shaming, and poor-shaming v. wealth-shaming. You will find liberals shaming liberals in the ongoing intersectionality wars, resulting in gay-on-gay shaming and black-on-black shaming.

Ain't that a shame? Yes, it is. It's a shame indeed, but don't expect the public shamers to feel ashamed of their public shaming. Have they no shame? No, not for themselves. Like all moralists, they exist only to shame others.

Public shaming is nothing new. It has long and ignoble history, from Roman crucifixions to the Spanish Inquisition to the "shame societies" of China (with its psychotic and murderous struggle sessions) and Japan (with its ritual of *seppuku* which, though self-directed, is often spurred by a suicidal sense of social shame). Every self-justifying social organism—i.e., *all* of them—puts its outliers and miscreants through some form of hairshirts , dunce caps, perp walks, and tarring and feathering, and they never seem to feel ashamed of indulging in such cruel and depressingly typical rituals, at least not while it's happening. Societies only seem capable of coming to terms with their collective potential for cruelty when it is too late to do anything about it. Thus, Americans still shed tears about Emmett Till and the Scottsboro Boys while turning a blind eye to modern black flash mobs.

Puritan New England remains infamous for its public stockades and witch trials and coldhearted shunning of anyone who dared deviate from the rigidly humorless social norm. This colonial culture of shaming was immortalized two centuries later in Nathaniel Hawthorne's *The Scarlet Letter*, where accused adulteress Hester Prynne was forced to wear a red "A" on her dress as a lifelong emblem of shame.

Those who foolishly believe that history is linear rather than cyclical seem to feel that we've progressed past such shaming rituals. After all, adultery is no longer a shunning offense; in some circles, it's a matter of pride.

And it's true that America's legal system no longer dunks witches in water or places offenders in the stocks for passersby to hurl rotten fruit at them. But it still exists in the form of judges sentencing petty offenders to public-humiliation rituals where they are forced to stand in public wearing sandwich boards declaring their crime.

Outside the legal system, our reputedly "progressive" society has merely swapped out the scarlet "A" for a scarlet "R," a scarlet "S," and a scarlet "H"—sometimes all three at once. Racism, sexism, and homophobia are now deemed to be as sinful as adultery was in the 1800s. Modern social-justice warriors, those little mob-motivated creeps, justify their behavior with the excuse that at least *this* time around, they're fighting for an irrefutably righteous cause.

Sure. That's what they *all* say.

What makes Internet-directed public shaming more insidious and cowardly than all prior forms is its ability to muster a million torch-bearers at once, none of whom is required to face their target in the flesh and look him in the eyes.

Thus you have little beta twerps such as the alleged male who runs something called "Public Shaming" on Tumblr, Twitter, and Facebook, all of it ostensibly designed to induce shame in those who merely think differently than he does, but most of which probably only makes likeminded chicken-chested snark-babies feel good about themselves. "I'm not a social crusader," claims the man-child behind the Public Shaming project. "But there is social activism in [what I do]." Such social activism includes calling others "racist fucking shitheads," "repugnant little slimeballs," "xenophobic idiots," and in one case, "a vile monster void [sic] of emotion and compassion."

Yeah, he sounds *highly* compassionate. It's not like he's a clone in an endless assembly line of "humanists" who seem to spend most of their time dehumanizing others. Cookie-cutter prog blogs such as Gawker and Huffington Post even have metadata tags for the phrase "Public Shaming." These are the neo-Puritans, so blinded by their own smug sense of righteousness, they can't even see it.

Internet public shaming reaches its most nauseating and damaging level in the cases of parents who trot out their kids like little Salem witches for all the world to mock. At least dog-shaming doesn't work because dogs, bless them, feel no shame. But for parents to treat their own spawn like Hester Prynne in order to score social-righteousness points reminds me of the Frank Zappa line, "If your children ever find out how lame you really are, they'll murder you in your sleep"—and he said that decades before YouTube existed to immortalize parental lameness.

When I was about three or four, I said the word "shit" in front of my mother, who then forced me to stand and repeat the word "shit" uninterrupted for a half-hour. The end result was that I kept saying "shit" throughout my life while convinced that my mother was sadistic.

On my first day of first grade, two boys got into a fight out in the schoolyard, and to shame them, the nuns made them kiss each other in front of the entire class. I felt bad for the boys and concluded that the nuns were sadistic.

When examining human behavior, especially when it hinges around guilt, it's always wise to consider the ubiquity of psychological projection. Maybe those who make a habit of shaming others only do so because they're easily shamed themselves. I wonder to what degree the currently fashionable hatred of the rich has to do with feelings of shame for not being nearly so successful. I also wonder what amount of black rage about slavery—and the subsequent never-ending campaign to shame white people about it—involves a deep-rooted shame over the fact that it was so easy to enslave them.

Public shaming would only seem to work on those pitiable social creatures who respect and fear the public's opinion. If you don't respect the crowd, there's no shame in being ostracized. If a person has the merest sense of self beyond their social identity, public shaming will fail. Thus, there's no shame in my game.

25

My Brief Brush With A Hate-Crime Hoax

In the summer of 1996 I was busy writing a book that argued America's main cultural divide is one of class rather than race. I had received a hefty advance to write it, part of which I gave to a scruffy little meth-head—imagine baseball pitcher Randy Johnson, only three feet shorter—to rebuild the engine in my tiny rusty Toyota. He promised me he'd have the job done in a week.

Three months later, he still wasn't done. I had no transportation the whole time, so I began to feel antsy. One night I rented a car to cruise Portland bars for women. After a long, fruitless search, I wound up at a bar only a block from where I lived.

In 1992, Portland had been home to one of the most elaborate hate-crime hoaxes ever. It involved a black, wheelchair-bound lesbian with the eternally fantastic name of Azalea Cooley. Not only did she fake having cancer, she faked multiple hate crimes against herself until cops got suspicious and set up surveillance cameras that revealed she, not the Klan, was responsible for burning a cross on her back porch.

The neighborhood I lived in was called St. Johns, located on Portland's far northern tip. I had been able to buy a two-bedroom house there for only $65,000. Despite what college sociology professors might lead you to believe, many borderline-poor and working-class neighborhoods are far more racially mixed than are many college sociology classes.

This bar was no exception. Although only about a block away from the clubhouse for all-white biker gang the Gypsy Jokers, it hosted whites, blacks, Mexicans, and even a few of North Portland's more infamous Native American clans.

About fifteen minutes before closing time, two dudes sauntered into the bar, and I immediately got the gut feeling that they were looking for trouble. One was black, the other Mexican. This had zero to do with why I sensed they were looking for trouble; it was the malevolence in their eyes. Some people just enter bars radiating menace. After getting a glimpse at them, I paid them no further mind.

When last call was over and the lights went up and the bartender shouted at us all to skedaddle, I walked into the parking lot behind the bar, only to notice that the menacing-looking black dude was sitting up against my rent-a-car talking to a girl. She saw that I wanted to leave and told him to get up off the car.

He walked straight up to me. "Give me a ride home," he commanded.

"No," I said sharply. "I don't know you." If he'd have asked nicely, maybe I would have considered it, but it goes against my grain to take orders like that.

Moments later, a wrinkly old Willie Nelson-looking white guy, shitfaced drunk, walked up to me and said something like, "You're older than me."

I sort of nodded and realized the situation was rapidly getting weird.

I got in the car, cranked it up, looked in the rearview mirror, and noticed that the black dude's Mexican friend was standing about a foot behind my car, talking to someone and blocking my exit.

I opened my car door, looked back, and said impatiently, "Can you *please* move?"

He moved, but only to walk up to me as I sat in the driver's seat, clenching his fist and asking why I was disrespecting him.

He didn't have time to punch me, because his black friend tried crawling between me and the steering wheel into the car.

FUCK this. I elbowed him out of the car, jammed it into reverse, and peeled the fuck out of that parking lot.

At 2:30 in the morning in St. Johns, cops are apparently waiting on every corner to bust people. As I was speeding, I was stopped only five blocks away by a police cruiser. They phoned in my license plate. Apparently the incident in the bar's parking lot had already been reported. They handcuffed me, threw me in the back of the squad car, and drove me back to the bar's parking lot.

I hadn't even realized that in my haste to get the fuck away from that parking lot, I'd knocked over both Willie Nelson and the Mexican when I'd pushed the car into reverse.

After getting their stories, a cop leaned in to look at me in the back seat and said, "Mr. Goad, they say you were hurling racial epithets at them."

I was floored. Here I was, spending all summer writing an antigovernment book that passionately claimed race wasn't important and that class was, yet here was a government official saying I'd run over some people after calling them racist names. For a moment I honestly wondered whether it was some elaborate government setup. After all, in the book I had noted that MLK and Malcolm X were both gunned down not when they were making it racial, but after they'd started talking about *all* poor people regardless of color. Martin Luther King had started his Poor People's Campaign the same year he got shot. And Black Muslims murdered Malcolm X after he'd made a trip to Mecca and noticed he was praying alongside people of all colors. Not that anyone had even seen my book yet—but when you're sitting in the back of a cop car being falsely accused, you may be forgiven for getting a trifle paranoid.

For fuck's sake, I had elbowed a black dude and knocked over a Mexican *and* a white guy. It was a Rainbow Coalition of victims—nothing racial about it—whom I would have left alone if they hadn't been fucking with me so hard.

About five minutes later, the cop came back and said every independent witness to the scene said my accusers were lying. They all independently confirmed my side of the story. Thank FUCK there were witnesses. The cop uncuffed me and sent me on my way.

My trio of victims later tried unsuccessfully to sue me. I was told that one of them—I'm guessing Ol' Willie, because he seemed the drunkest—was so hammered that night, he had walked out of the emergency room before being treated.

But the experience left a bitter taste in my mouth and made me feel naïve for thinking that race wasn't important. It was *obviously* important to those who seemed to feel they could claim automatic victim status because of it. When you start with a blanket assumption that *any* group is operating from powerlessness and innocence, you invite a handful of manipulative psychopaths to take advantage of that presumption.

Thus, we live in a world that still largely denies that there are false accusations of rape, false accusations of gay-bashing, and false accusations of racist hatred (again and again and again). And it's this stupidly childish and ultimately patronizing presumption that members of historically oppressed groups could never be malicious themselves—in other words, that they are not truly human and capable of fucked-up behavior like anyone else is—that continues to impede what I'd like to define as true progress.

26

Skinheads Against White People

Blood pours from my nose as I stand on a downtown Portland street corner, arguing with antiracist skinheads about grammar.

"Why the FUCK did you have to hit me?" I implore the half-dozen halfwits half my age who surround me. "If you had a problem with me, why couldn't you TALK about it? Fuck, I'll spot any one of you 40 IQ points and still outargue you!"

"Dumbass—'outargue' isn't a word," one of them smirks.

"It's in the DICTIONARY! It's one word! It's not even a HYPHENATE!" I scream.

I wipe my face. Both my palms are covered in my own blood. One of the muttonchopped Brit clones had sucker-punched me while I was in a nondefensive position.

I had been standing outside a nightclub's pizza window with my severely Jewish-looking Jew girlfriend when I first espied the six skins and a pair of skinettes eyeballing my iron cross necklace.

I identified them as the Rose City Bovver Boys, a rootin', tootin', pathologically antiracist skinhead crew who boast one

Vietnamese member to deflect attention from the fact that the rest of them are the color of Ivory soap. They claim to no longer be affiliated with the Skinheads Against Racial Prejudice movement, yet I've never heard of them bum-rushing anyone for reasons other than nigger-hating or telling Jew jokes.

"What's with the iron cross?" a simian-looking and extravagantly stupid white boy who goes by the online handle "Mattie Valentine" finally grilled me.

"It's a white thing," I said sarcastically. "Why don't you punch me for it?"

"That's fucked-up," he grunted.

"Yeah, man—you can make a name for yourself. My name is Jim Goad, and if you hit me, it'll be in every paper in the city."

"I'd like to be the guy who beats Jim Goad up," he said a microsecond before smashing my nose with his right fist.

As the blood started flowing, I looked down the street and saw a cop car about two blocks away. Unlike any of these young rebel skinheads, I'd been to prison and was on parole.

"What the fuck is your problem, anyway?" I ask as they swarm around me. "You all hate yourselves for being white?"

"I'm not white," one of the white boys says.

"Bitch, if you went to prison, I'll bet the brothers would think you're white."

My big-schnozzed girlfriend is screaming that she's Jewish and I'm not a Nazi and what the fuck what the fuck what the fuck?!?—a dozen years prior, she was the one who dropped a dime to the FBI, ratting out the Nazi skins who'd beaten an Ethiopian man to death with baseball bats—a crime from which lily-white Portland, the most Caucasian metro area in the USA, still feels the need to "heal" itself. In essence, she'd done more for the SHARP cause than they could ever do.

Still surrounded by a half-dozen short-haired mosquitoes, I now see clearly that my only option is to fight. I crack my assailant with an Earnie Shavers-style left hook, staggering him. I land three or four clean punches to his head, while all he can do is tear at my T-shirt like a bitch.

A cop car pulls up and we all scatter. All except the two skinettes, who lie to the police that it started when some assholes were shouting racist things.

I felt super-macho for days. A golfball-size lump formed on my left-hand middle finger, where I'd slammed his head.

"Goddamn, let me think twice before messing with you!" the club's security guard later laughed. "I've NEVER seen a left hook like that! You left a dent in that boy's head!"

Yes, sir. And I didn't feel guilty about it. I was furious. For all my alleged fascism, I'd NEVER harassed anyone based on their race, gender, sexual orientation, or fashion choices. It was a simple fucking IRON CROSS. And even if I'd been wearing a goddamned Flavor Flav swastika clock hanging down to my balls, it was NOBODY'S business to try and bully me about it.

A few days later, I see a wheelchair-bound black homeless man who'd witnessed the fight. "Why were those Nazis bothering you?" he asks me.

"They aren't Nazis," I tell him. "They thought I was a Nazi."

He's confused. As am I. As is the rest of the world.

I first heard of Skinheads Against Racial Prejudice in the early 90s. Defining themselves as the antidote to Nazi skins, they claim to be the "true" skinheads, reclaiming a tradition the racists had perverted. They operate from the assumption that it is possible—righteous, even—to beat someone into embracing racial tolerance. The SHARPies argue that you can't argue with Nazis—that Nazis only understand violence—and they have been proactive in routing white-power elements from the nearly all-white punk-rock scene.

But despite their name, you won't find SHARPs attacking members of the Nation of Islam, who clearly preach racial prejudice. No, their beef is entirely with white people—or, for the ones who believe race is only an ideological construct, with the IDEA of whiteness. Only whites can be racist, goes their thinking, so only whites deserve to have their noses broken for it—by other whites, of course, who aren't being patronizing to black people or Jews at all by acting as their surrogate Defense League.

The SHARPs believe it's horrible to harass people for their skin color but MANDATORY to bully them over their alleged beliefs. A terrible thing to exterminate racial "scum" but a sacred duty to wipe out ideological "scum." Their antifascist rhetoric is amusingly fascistic. SMASH the Nazis with the Fist of Solidarity! LYNCH the racist scum! Don't let the sun set on you in THIS town, Nazi!

In Portland—once known as skinhead capital of the U.S.—SHARPs staged several strategic battles with racist skin gangs such as East Side White Pride. In 1993, Eric Banks, singer for white-power band Bound for Glory, was shot dead on the P-town streets by SHARP associates.

Banks's murder didn't get nearly as much publicity as the Nazis' baseball-bat bludgeoning of the Ethiopian, because as we all know, human lives are NOT equal, and the life of a white, male American Nazi is CLEARLY not worth as much as an Ethiopian immigrant's. We all know this to be a fact, so let's not even GO there.

In Portland, the antiracist skins were perhaps a little TOO successful in their mission. I moved here in '94. Ten years later, to my touristy disappointment, I've yet to see a single Nazi skinhead anywhere in town.

And because there are no real Nazis left, the SHARPs had to broadly expand their definition of what constitutes a Nazi in order to justify their existence.

Greasers, since they embraced a style from the segregation era, became prime targets for lopsided SHARPie beatdowns. So did skateboarders who wore the Independent logo with its evil iron cross. Really, anyone who made eye contact with them and didn't cower—or whatever intrepid soul dared question their thuggish Stalinist tactics—became an automatic Nazi worthy of a pummeling.

I've heard one story after the next of the Rose City boys smashing pint glasses in faces, holding a knife to a girl's throat, kicking a kid in the face when he was already down, and beating the brains out of a skinny German teen because he wasn't ashamed of being German.

And despite all the violence, and regardless of their loudly barked anticop stance, what's queer is that they hardly ever get arrested. Some have murmured that they must have friends in high places, sympathetic string pullers willing to allow just about any act of antiracist hooliganism so long as Portland's streets are kept Nazi-free.

See, it's like this—although they pose as street warriors bravely fighting a racist society, the truth is that SHARPs operate with society's overwhelming sympathy—all the news outlets, all the courts, all but a paltry handful of psychopathic racist nutjobs are APPALLED by Nazis to the point where they believe murder is too good for 'em.

In 2004, you risk very little by saying you hate Nazis. It's such a popular stance, it borders on cowardly.

The bottom line is that SHARPs enjoy the homoerotic rush of boys bonding together through crisp uniforms and manly blood oaths, of sublimating their Rosicrucian cumlust through the orgiastic ritual of joining together and attacking another male's body.

Nothing wrong with that, really.

What's despicable is that they just can't come out and admit it. Instead, they hide behind the risk-free shield of anti-racism, the last refuge of scoundrels.

A few days after my initial run-in with the anti-Nazis—also, ironically, a few days after a white-power website accused me of being a Jew lover and a race traitor—a representative of the Rose City skins meets with me and explains that his gang has no beef with me—it was merely a personal thing between me and the sucker-puncher, who had read my work and decided I was a "sick" individual who needed to be killed. Sucker-punch boy had told his homies I'd written about how I enjoyed "beating the Jew" out of my wife.

"That's ludicrous!" I say, resentful that I even have to explain myself. "I'll give you my books—you can see for yourself. I've never written anything remotely like that. My book *The Redneck Manifesto* is the most nonracist book in the world—it argues that class, not race, is what's important."

"I don't want to read your stuff," he says, almost wary that it might rub off on him. "All you had to do was take off that iron cross, and everything would have been OK."

"But that's just the point—nobody appointed you the police. Fuck, you guys dress all British, and that's the most racist nation in history! It wasn't the Americans who enslaved Africa and colonized India and China. And while we're on the topic, I'm Irish, and frankly, I'm a little offended by your UK fetish. But the difference between me and you is that I don't dictate what you should wear. So who's the real asshole here? Who's the real fascist? Again, if any of you have a problem with me, I'm always available for a debate. I love to argue ideas."

"Some things are NOT open for debate," he says ominously. "WE were the ones who put the shackles on the black man's ankles, and WE were the ones who brought them here."

I don't know how old this cat was, but I sure as fuck wasn't alive when all that shit went down. And I'm not going to swallow a guilt trip for crimes I didn't commit. Guess that makes me an automatic Nazi, huh?

Nearly a year later, I'm invited to a friend's bar to introduce another friend's band when nine or so Rose City boys show up and begin vibing the room. A couple of them bump into me on purpose.

Normally neurotic and skittish, but a fearless lion in the face of danger, I walk straight up to them and ask what's up.

"You're a piece of shit," says their leader, a balding, short-but-thick man in his 30s named Pan Nesbitt. A lifelong police informant, Nesbitt snitched out his own partner in the murder of

Eric Banks and avoided jail time. When Nazi skin Randall Krager called him and threatened him by phone, Pan ran to the police and had Krager jailed for a crime known in Oregon as Intimidation.

Pan claims to be Jewish and wears a Star of David necklace which—surprisingly, since I'm supposed to be a Nazi—I don't demand that he remove.

"Oh, I'm a piece of shit?" I say. "So, I'm scum? So, I'm worthless? So, I need to be exterminated? Funny, that's how Nazis used to look at Jews."

"You're a sad man," he says, getting nose-to-nose.

"Sometimes I'm happy, sometimes I'm sad."

"I know who I am," he announces with dumb pride.

"I know who I am, too," I counter, "and I don't need to be surrounded by nine guys to prove it."

"You're a nobody," he tells me, his uncomprehending, beady eyes flaring with anger.

"I'm known around the world," I say. "You're only known by your road dogs and maybe a dozen other people in this town."

"You can't even argue with me on a logistical level," he proclaims.

"You're a moron and can't even use words properly," I tell him.

Unable to argue, he head-butts me. But it doesn't hurt. It doesn't even break the skin. I have the hardest head on earth.

I'm still on parole. I'm not going to fight nine guys. I'm not going back to prison over some clowns who can't even articulate why they hate me.

The Armenian bar owner asks Jewskin why he head-butted me.

"He doesn't like black people," the Jewskin lies.

"Well, I'm a sand nigger," says the bar owner. "Are you going to hit me, too?"

Yes. The bar erupts into a brawl. I leave before the cops arrive.

The Portland police consider the Rose City skins to be Oregon's second-largest gang. Their "logistical" leader is suspected by police to be the primary shooter in one homicide and an accomplice in several attempted homicides. In 1992, he beat a 16-year-old alleged Nazi kid into a coma, causing permanent brain damage (in the kid—not sure what caused the assailant's obvious brain damage).

A few months later, I see fat, bald Jewskin and two of his henchmen outside another downtown Portland club. A manic-depressive, black cowboy date-rapist had tipped them off to my presence there. When I spot the Jewskin, I tell my friends to go inside.

"Hey, Goad, you don't like me and I don't like you," he says, walking up to me.

"Yeah, that about sums it up."

He sucker-punches me. A clean shot to the temple. I've been hit a lot harder. He has a rep as a badass, but maybe he's losing his touch.

"You know I'm on parole and I'm not going to risk fighting on the streets again," I tell him. "But I will fight you in a boxing ring—just as long as I get to debate you first and prove to the world what a MORON you are."

"I'm not too good on the lyrical skills," he says, admitting that perhaps he's stupid, "but let's go around the corner and I'll show you what I got."

"Again—I'm not going to get busted because of you. For some weird reason, the cops don't arrest you guys. But I'll fight you in a boxing ring as long as I get to fight you with words first."

And that's when I saw a familiar look in his eyes.

HATRED.

Blind, dumb, animal hatred. The hatred of fools. The hatred of subhumans.

You can't fight hatred with more hatred. And you can't fight Nazis by acting like a Nazi. It just turns the whole world into Nazis.

I'm off parole now, so the game has changed. I'm not nearly as hesitant to defend myself should the need arise.

I've been beat up dozens of times. No big deal. But if you beat me up, what does that prove? That might is right? That's a Nazi idea, G.

My politics? I'm a Goad Supremacist. I've had my ass kicked, but I've never lost an argument. So if you're fighting over ideas—if you're really something more than dumb thugs—why can't you act like men and DISCUSS those ideas? Send me your brightest mind—your sharpest SHARP—and watch me turn him into a monkey. I don't hate Jews or blacks, but I hate hypocrites. I hate people who hide behind a "good" cause to do their dirty work.

I want to know what we're fighting for. If it's free speech, then I'll fight. If it's the right to think and wear whatever I want, then I'll fight for that, too. I just won't fight for Hitler. My new Jewish girlfriend wouldn't approve.

27

A Blizzard Of
Special Snowflakes

It wasn't quite the Kent State Massacre, but you wouldn't know it from the students' anguished wails.

Last Monday morning, students at Emory University here in Atlanta were emotionally triggered by messages scrawled in chalk throughout the campus. The messages were so horrifying and terrifying that by the afternoon a gaggle of 40 or so students stormed the Administration Building and began desperately chanting:

You are not listening! Come speak to us, we are in pain!...We have nothing to lose but our chains.

What exactly had sent them into such blind, flailing, fearful fury? Well, it wasn't exactly Kristallnacht, but let's call it "The Chalkening": A vandal had scrawled "TRUMP 2016" on signs and stairs and walkways throughout this tony campus where parents waste a quarter-million dollars to send their progeny for a four-year course in how to be a soft-boiled ovum or a walking mangina.

A blogger for snopes.com claimed that numerous reports of students' hysterical reactions to The Chalkening were "MOSTLY FALSE," but I'll provide some direct quotes from the quivering pupils themselves and let you decide:

"This wasn't ordinary campaigning. It was deliberate intimidation. Some of us were expecting shootings. We feared walking alone....To us, the administration's silence sanctioned the fact that this Nazi reincarnate [Trump] is threatening to deport our parents—to put us in concentration camps and kill us."

—Sophomore Jonathan Peraza, pictured here leading easily aggrieved students in a round of collective self-pity

"I'm supposed to feel comfortable and safe [here]. But this man [Trump] is being supported by students on our campus and our administration shows that they, by their silence, support it as well....I don't deserve to feel afraid at my school."

—Unnamed student quoted in school paper the *Emory Wheel*

"[Faculty] are supporting this rhetoric by not ending it...people of color are struggling academically because they are so focused on trying to have a safe community and focus on these issues [related to having safe spaces on campus]."

—Another unnamed student quoted in the *Emory Wheel* who appears to not have ever considered that certain groups of color's low mean IQ might be a contributing factor in their academic struggles

"My reaction to the chalking was one of fear....People still don't understand that the protest yesterday served not only as an expression against one interpretation of the chalking, but also as a collective manifestation against the fear that a bigot leader can create.

—Freshman Amanda Obando

"I legitimately feared for my life. I thought we were having a KKK rally on campus."

—Freshman Paula Camila Alarcon, quoted in the Daily Beast

"I think it was an act of violence. It was an active threat, intentionally meant to create opposition on campus and to segregate groups on

campus that are already segregated."
—Junior Lolade Oshin, also quoted in the Daily Beast

Behold the sad, glum faces of these easily triggered ambulatory fetuses, fearing they'll be shipped back to truly "safe spaces" such as Mexico or the Middle East. Each one of them appears to be a flaming pain in the ass—an "Emorrhoid," if you will.

Such mass eruptions of colicky college students are nothing new, although The Chalkening may mark a new level of absurdity. Last year University of Missouri president Tim Wolfe stepped down after black students threw a collective fit when a fecal swastika was spotted on campus and the black Student Body President falsely reported that the KKK was prowling the campus.

During the Mizzou nonsense, a black grad student went on a hunger strike to protest the oppression he allegedly suffered at the school merely for being black, even though in 2014 his daddy had raked in a cool $8.4 million in earnings.

I would *kill* to be so oppressed. And although Butler reportedly began stuffing his face mere minutes after the university president resigned, I believe I have the patience and fortitude to sit and calmly watch a hunger striker starve to death.

Also last year, a Japanese student at Oberlin wrote a scathing article about how the school cafeteria's sushi was "appropriative." At California's Claremont McKenna College, the Dean of Students resigned after penning an apparently sincere email to a Latina student offering to help those who "don't fit our...mold." And a Yale lecturer who'd sent an email urging students to quit freaking the hell out over allegedly "offensive" Halloween costumes resigned amid the belching outrage that ensued, which included a shrieking She-gro publicly bitching out the lecturer's hubby.

In 2014, a Muslim student who'd poked fun at the very idea of "trigger warnings" for a conservative paper at the University of Michigan found his apartment doorway vandalized with eggs and hot dogs, along with scribbled notes such as "SHUT THE FUCK UP" and "EVERYONE HATES YOU, YOU VIOLENT PRICK."

In 2008 a white student at Purdue was found guilty of racial harassment for reading an *anti*-KKK book because a co-worker found the book cover's depiction of a Klan rally to be emotionally intolerable.

And then there's 1993's infamous "Water buffalo incident" at the University of Pennsylvania, where a group of loud and disruptive black females went sobbing to officials after being told to keep their voices down.

Whenever I hear about such incidents, the immediate question that springs to mind is, "How *easy* have their lives been for them to be acting like this?"

When they equate words—especially non-threatening ones—with "violence," which they seem to be doing with increasing fecklessness, I wonder if anyone has ever punched them square in the mouth. I know the difference between real violence and words. I've been on both the giving and receiving ends of *literal* violence throughout much of my life, including early childhood. These wilted orchids don't seem to have a clue, or they wouldn't conflate words and deeds.

From my vantage point, this is not the behavior of people who've been oppressed; these are convenient and dictatorial temper tantrums from post-pubescent infants who have been spoiled beyond all reason. Maybe they aren't fragile at all—perchance they're tyrants hiding behind a facade of weakness in order to acquire power and bludgeon others with it. One is tempted to really give them something to cry about.

When they are disgorged like fetal cannonballs from the warm womb of modern college life, one would hope they quickly learn the meaning of real pain and suffering. I would like nothing more than to peer out my window one day and watch all these special snowflakes melt the moment they hit the ground.

28

Bay Aryan Resistance

San Francisco constantly struggles with itself to solve the question of how many assholes it's possible to fit into a square mile. How many cybersissies can you cram into a phone booth? How many Gaia-peddling belly-floppers? How many self-absorbed monkish Nerf balls of ideological irrelevance? How many Day-Glo lemon-meringue fashion tarantulas? How many gaunt, cellophane-wrapped nipple-tweakers? How many prune-twatted hipster debutantes?

It's a star-lit ballroom full of elitists masquerading as egalitarians. Of snobs pretending to be socialists. Of petty backstabbers who appoint themselves as moral crusaders. These creeps can't get along with the other 99% of the country—shit, most of their time is spent quarreling among *themselves*—yet they try to fist-fuck you with Universal Brotherhood.

Almost down to the very last shaved anus, San Franciscans are a xenophobic breed. If you don't speak, look, and act like a San Franciscan, their policy is one of Zero Tolerance. They're totalitarian in the sense that they insist on controlling the thoughts and lives of others through forceful statist intervention. In doing so, they align themselves with the establishment which they pretend to be overthrowing. They're a buncha urban supremacists. Unyielding. Humorless. Stuffed to the gills with an unwarranted sense of their own cultural/moral superiority. I call them "Bay Aryans."

Surely I must be kidding, that I don't mean to compare such twinkle-toed West Coast coolness-mongerers to the TEETH-CHATTERINGLY SINISTER ATROCITIES of the Nazi pork-butchers. After all, Hitler killed six million Jewboys! That's enuff goldurned Heeb-a-roos to fill eight San Franciscos. You may be right, Tootsie Pop, but are you aware that non-racist, peace-licking, universal-personhood-touting communist governments slaughtered an estimated ONE HUNDRED AND TWENTY MILLION PEOPLE in the 20th century? The commies beat Hitler 20-1. Their unbounded love for "humanity" didn't seem to put a check on an even stronger love for controlling and killing human beings. So much for your murky notions of government-mandated humanism. Better a Nazi than a commie, I guess.

And either one's better than a Bay Aryan. Being born in San Francisco is excusable, provided that you evacuate within 30 days of reaching adulthood. But moving TO the Bay Area is unforgivable under any circumstance. Based on an unfortunate long-term trend of Freak Relocation, the town has become a sort of Kurdish tent village of refugee weirdlings. A once-pretty city with happy-flappy seagulls has degenerated into an island of whitebreads-in-exile who've all fled from hometown persecution. San Francisco's foggy hills have become America's Largest Support Group, a Jonestown for people who were socially traumatized in high school. Within city limits, I think San Francisco's fine as a cultural sanctuary for oversocialized misfits. Its danger lies in an apparently insatiable drive to vengefully impose its values on everyone outside the fortress. I think it's good that you people should have your own ghetto. I just think we should build a fence around it.

Among most humans, the need for social approval seems stronger than the desire to know the truth. Rejected by the Über-clique, the Bay Aryans form cliques of their own. Blind puppies in a cardboard box, they crawl over each other groping for "scene" status. They are so weak as individuals, they truly believe that "scene" status is a worthwhile goal. They howl about "fighting fascism," yet they exhibit a strong urge to feel part of some "community," which is the first flash of the fascist impulse.

You all need a crowd. You all need a movement. You need to be surrounded by the wool of a million other sheep before you finally feel warm. You all have social consciences because you're zeros as individuals. Your compassion for others is ironically founded on your own self-hatred. You swim with "the movement" because you're lost on your own.

I don't care about your precious personal lifestyle choices. I really don't. And your entire dingbat philosophy, the whole tectonic plate upon which San Francisco rests, is based on the false presumption that people such as me are somehow upset about the manner in which you flap your genitals around. Egads.

It isn't what you do, it's the way you do it. Not the meat, but rather the motion. It's not what you're saying, it's your lousy voice. It isn't your private cock-slurping, it's your public megaphone-mouth. It ain't how you move beneath the sheets, it's the way you wave the picket signs around. The problem isn't your self-consciously "decadent" personal lifestyle, It's your warped social instincts.

It has nothing to do with the widespread sidewalk displays of ass-rimming...or the women who look like Lou Costello...or even the concept of white people who hate the concept of white people. In fact, those are some of the things I LIKE about SF. It's the attitude. The vantage point. Cloistered in a cultural Presidio, the Bay Aryans see fit to cast judgment about the millions of peasants who live out on the Plains.

The Bay Aryans prove that they aren't truly compassionate by consistently showing a flagrant hatred for America's white rural lumpenproletariat. Though San Franciscans may mince through the streets in protest of hate speech, they sure as shootin' despise dem trailer trash. Although their hearts are opened like dilated rectums for poster kids halfway around the world, they disowned the homebound hillbillies a long time ago. I wonder what would happen if the hillbillies were to disown the Bay Aryans? Maybe if all the redneck farmers just decided to stop growing crops for a year. Perhaps if all the white-trash truckers agreed to halt delivery of all goods into this hostile enemy area. Maybe if all the Evil White Male Pig cops decided to ease up on Oakland and let black people REALLY express how they feel about their brethren in Frisco and Berkeley. That's all it would take. A puff of wind, and they'd all fall down.

It's a good thing that the rest of the country sees your city as a harmless Fruitcake Palace. The rest of America is too busy trying to put food on the table than worrying about your neurotic socio-libidinal peccadilloes. The rest of America could get along fine without San Francisco. The reverse is hardly true.

You should thank Goddess that there are a few Nazis in Idaho and a smattering of Klansmen in Kentucky, because what else would you talk about at the weekly gatherings of the collective? Never mind that you all live in a much more AFFLUENT place than Idahoans or Kentuckians do.

Personal finances don't often factor into your ideas of what constitutes oppression, do they? You claim to identify with the poor and downtrodden, yet you're miraculously able to pay some of the highest rents in America. How do you do it? Maybe if you took the silver spoon out of your mouth, I'd be able to understand what you were mumbling about empowerment.

Modern American Leftoidism, a *Volk* religion epitomized in places such as the evil SF/Berkeley vortex, is almost exclusively the purview of upper-middle-class white kids who've never breathed a fleeting gasp of true oppression in their lives. This must be why the Bay Aryans don't seem nearly as concerned with America's widening class disparities as they are with its fashion mistakes and verbal boorishness. Though the Bay Aryans fancy themselves as revolutionaries, they're actually little more than a left-wristed inversion of Miss Manners. An area that prides itself on the Free Speech Movement is now gung-ho in favor of legal restrictions on terminology which it doesn't deem proper or sensitive. The Bay area teems with tattletales and stool pigeons and hall monitors and snitches. Since they don't have any REAL problems in their lives, these mushy bananas worry about getting their feelings bruised.

Perhaps it hasn't occurred to you, but human history is not *entirely* summarized by the bold struggle for the "right" to poke your veiny ding-dong through disco-bathroom glory holes. Not every act is political. Some are just silly and ugly and stinky.

Are you all high on crack? Does some municipal law require you to either have a glass pipe or a dick in your mouth at all times? Who else would seriously try to argue that rape has nothing to do with sex or that racism has nothing to do with economics? The holes in your logic have been stretched wider than your sphincters. Any honest overview of African, Asian, and Hispanic cultures would reveal more sexism, homophobia, and ethnic strife than you could shake a white dick at. Everyone is born corrupt. White males were simply better at it.

You can show your sincere opposition to white-male imperialism by giving your city back to the Injuns. Maybe we could help San Francisco realize its multicultural dreams by immediately shipping a million or so Third World indigents there. Let them take your jobs while *you* starve for a while. We could forcibly relocate all the white-hipster undesirables out to Alcatraz, where they'd perform bloody gladitorial feats to the delight of Kenyan tourists on paddleboats.

I'm glad you've all gathered together in one place. Makes it easier to aim the missiles. Aren't you due for another natural disaster or something? Exactly what year are you scheduled to slide into the ocean? I want to take pictures.

No offense, but I have a higher opinion of the runny, worm-filled dogshit I scrape from my boot with a Popsicle stick than I do of your fair city. You gave us OJ Simpson, but what have you done lately?

San Francisco, America's B-movie imitation of Paris.

San Francisco, the city that ruined punk rock.

San Francisco, the most intolerant place in the country.

Second to Berkeley, of course. Berkeley's so bad, it's too painful to talk about.

Tony Bennett left his heart. I took a dump. I'd tell you all to go to hell, but you already live there.

29

A Vast White-Wing Conspiracy

Book review: Richard Dyer, *WHITE*. New York: Routledge Press, 1997.

Imagine if Hitler was secretly Jewish and owned a publishing company that released several books with the word 'Jew' in the title. Routledge Press, which I'm guessing is owned by whites, makes a habit of doing the same thing with the word 'white.' They've released *Whitewash*, *Off White*, *White Lies*, *White Mythologies*, *How the Irish Became White*, and then, just to keep it simple, a book merely called *WHITE*. In all of these, 'white' roughly translates as 'evil.' All of these books make the mistake of portraying Whiteness as Monolith, as if social classes never existed.

In *WHITE*, white man Richard Dyer says things about whites than in any other ethnic context would be seen as virulently racist. He mentions "the dead end of whiteness" and states that "whites are nothing and have had their day, that we are, and perhaps always have been, the dead...being nothing, having no life, is a condition of whiteness." He refers to "white male paranoia" and its "mania for measurable biological distinctions." Hey, dude, it's better than playing with rocks and swatting at flies.

To him, everything is "ethnically suggestive," and race "is never not a factor, never not in play." He is that latter-day oxymoron, an anti-racist who can only think in racial terms.

As a gay white man, he's especially snippy toward white women, alleging that most of them lead "contemptibly empty lives." He calls heterosexuality "the cradle of whiteness," as if black, Latin, and Asian cultures were relatively queer-friendly. Yes, in the 'hood, they're just ga-ga over fey British Nancy-boys. As Professor Griff once alleged (paraphrased), "The African language [sic] doesn't even have a word for 'homosexual.'" The difference between black women and white women? The sistas would call Dyer "shaky" rather than "queer." That's about it.

Dyer says, "I am not ashamed to think white masculinity a menace," yet I must conclude that he's not at all threatened when black males act butch. He admits to having the hots for nonwhites and reveals his belief that blacks are better at fucking and dancing than whites. How 'bout calculus? Nation-building? Scientific invention beyond finding new ways to use the peanut? Any thoughts on those things?

There are so many contradictions, this white boy doesn't know where to start. Dyer apparently believes something is true so long as he wishes it were so. He calls black-on-white rape a "trope," something confined to "racist fictions," yet he mentions "the routinised misuse of non-white women by white men." Holy moly, I wonder if he's seen the 1988 FBI Uniform Crime Reports, which state that of 9,415 interracial rapes that year, only TEN were white-on-black? Biting himself in the ass yet again, he calls fascism "an avowedly white form of politics," pretending that there was never a Pol Pot, Idi Amin, or Somoza.

He has a good point when he states that many whites see themselves as non-racial and ordinary rather than a distinct ethnic group, broadly alleging that "all white people in the West do this all the time." Yet he fails to address the fact that ALL cultures, not just European ones, portray themselves as the center of the universe.

He wastes something like sixty pages talking about how photography and film making "privileges white people in the image" and that "movie lighting discriminates against non-white people," yet he can't seem to explain why nonwhites haven't invented their own photographic techniques with which to flatter themselves. He even proposes that the Tarzan movies were in black-and-white because color would suggest "coloured people." You think I'm making this shit up?

Stylistically, he's even more annoying than I am. Dyer, an earnest queer, earnestly queries,

> If I continue to see whiteness only in texts in which there are also non-white people, am I not reproducing the relegation of non-white people to the function of enabling me to understand myself?

Shut the fuck up. Really. Go dig some ditches or lay some telephone cable for a while, and them come back to me talking about privilege.

Regarding this nebulous thing the kids call whiteness, he avers,

> It is carried by signs of pastness and a geographical location, whose imprecision in no way diminishes the mobilisation of an historical imagination.

Huh? Whazzat? Come again? Try popping that shit in the South Bronx or Compton, and see how warmly you're embraced. Black people don't read these sort of books, G.

Dyer also has a proclivity for the unnecessary self-referential phrase, such as, "already touched on in Chapter 1," or "to be discussed in Chapter 6." And when he states, "Let me provide some instances of this," I wonder what would happen if I said, "No—stop it—I'm not going to let you."

Sometimes it's wise to reveal your personal background,

sometimes it isn't. Dyer makes the mistake of uncovering the true root of his ethnic self-loathing: In the mid-seventies, while solo-dancing between two lines of racially mixed friends à la *Soul Train*, he recalls feeling very gawky and white. So because he's a lousy dancer, he yearns for the collapse of white civilization. He doesn't realize that even if this were to happen, he *still* couldn't dance. He also reveals he hates whiteness because his white childhood peers treated him as a sissy-freak. One can only assume that if he were born black, he'd be a self-hating Oreo decrying brutish gangstas to some empathetic Ofay who enjoys rubbing ashen elbows with the Talented Tenth.

Richard Dyer is a white man who wants to be black, which I'm sure makes black people very happy and grateful. Ooh, the joy—another white guy pretending he's not white. Get it through your ganja-soaked heads—self-hatred, in any flavor, is the sign of a masochistic psychological complex rather than political insight.

30

A Handy Guide To Popular Social Justice Hashtags (And What They Really Mean)

As everyone with two brain cells to rub together is well aware, a tremendous amount of social injustice exists in this so-called world of ours. To rectify this unfortunate situation, many among us who are devoted to enforcing equality by all means necessary have taken to wielding our smartphones like *Star Wars* lightsabers against all the big fat mean rich white male capitalist sexist scum-sucking cisgender pigs who need to be brutally tortured in public and then wiped off the planet because they think it's cool and funny to dehumanize others.

Hashtag activism is a relatively new weapon in the arsenal of social justice warriors who seek to erase national borders, do away with greed, abolish ethnic conflict, eradicate hate speech, criminalize transphobia, foster a harmonious global community under one benevolent governmental taxing agency, and all other manner of, like, totally realistic and absolutely plausible goals.

From the comfort of their dorm rooms and mothers' basements all across this bounteous planet, they largely take to Twitter, which with its 140-character limit per post is tailor-made for oversimplified solutions that appeal to people with short attention spans. A "hashtag" uses the pound sign, AKA the tic-tac-toe sign, followed by a short phrase—for example, #HashtagsAreStupid. Once a sufficient number of people use that hashtag in their Tweets, it becomes a "trending topic" and allows everyone who uses it to feel as if they are important and part of something greater than themselves—which is especially soothing to people who don't feel they're that great in the first place.

As a social-justice hashtag activist, you can invade someone's privacy, get them fired, encourage lynch-mob bullying tactics, shut down dissenting opinions, and feel like a good person all at the same time.

Herewith is a handy guide to some of the more popular social justice hashtags of the past few years.

* * * * * * * * * * * *

#BringBackOurGirls

By all accounts, Nigeria is a fun place full of child witches, penis panics, killer phone calls, and car thieves who transform themselves into goats. But this vibrant and sprawling African nation also harbors the gun-toting Islamic militant group Boko Haram, who are most famous for their late-1960s classic-rock hit "A Whiter Shade of Pale." Never mind the fact that early in 2014 Boko Haram had already killed about 1,000 Nigerians—most of them young males, some of whom were burned alive. No, the news story that captured the large hearts and tiny minds of hashtag activists was the kidnapping of some 200 schoolgirls and their forced conversion to Islam. Thus was born the hashtag #BringBackOurGirls, which was retweeted around two million times. First Lady Michelle Obama even frowningly posed for a selfie holding a placard that said BRING BACK OUR GIRLS.

As of this writing, our girls have yet to be brought back.

* * * * * * * * * * * *

#Kony2012

Even though he's black, Joseph Kony is a bad, bad, EVIL African militia leader who helmed the Lord's Resistance Army and became a fugitive of the International Criminal Court. In 2012, a slacktivist named Jason Russell produced a half-hour video which at the time became the most viral video in Internet history and currently has been viewed on YouTube over 100 million times. The video called for the capture of this Black Hitler by the end of 2012. Jason Russell was quoted as saying, "We can have fun while we end genocide." He even suggested producing T-shirts that read AFRICA IS SO HOT RIGHT NOW and AFRICA IS THE NEW PINK. However, at the height of his cheap fame, it was Russell rather than Kony whom police captured. It seems he became "dehydrated" and did what any sane dehydrated person would do—he tore off all his clothing and ran around naked in Pacific Beach, CA, taunting passersby. Russell has faded into a well-deserved obscurity while Joseph Kony remains at large.

* * * * * * * * * * * *

#BlackLivesMatter

Black Americans enjoy a far higher standard of living and live much longer than blacks in any majority-black nation on Earth. Black males comprise about 6% of the American population and routinely commit more than half of America's homicides. During any given year, police kill about twice as many white Americans than they kill black Americans. And in the vast majority of these cases, the "victims" were armed. Oh—and around 93% of black murder victims are killed by other blacks, not by police.

But none of this matters to Black Lives Matter.

Their troglodytic rage is directed at the relatively tiny number of yearly murders in which a white cop kills a black person. They remove all mitigating circumstances—such as, you know, whether the lumbering beast of the mid-American Plains was grabbing for the cop's gun rather than peacefully holding his hands up and begging the cop not to shoot him—and use such statistical anomalies and outright fabrications to loot and pillage and burn their cities to the ground. And what happens in cities such as Baltimore and Ferguson after the Black Lives Matter creeps leave nothing but a scorched carcass of a metropolitan wasteland? The cops back off, businesses move out, and more black people kill one another than ever.

* * * * * * * * * * * *

#StopGamergate

Since feminist activists are fanatics, and since fanatics can't keep their beaks out of anyone else's business until everyone is either scared into silence or as fanatical as they are, the squalling harpies of female supremacy began infiltrating the once musty, dudely realms of video gaming to inject feminist messages that promote a feminist narrative and make boys feel ashamed to be sexually aroused by "sexist" (i.e., attractive) images of scantily clad females being rescued by impossibly muscular video-game he-men.

The original "reaction" to this full-frontal pudendal assault was dubbed "GamerGate" and initially had something or other to do with some girl allegedly using her female wiles to seduce a male gaming writer into giving her game a good review. It was about "ethics in gaming journalism" or some such. Mind you, that's from memory—it's all so annoying at this point that I can't even be bothered to check the specifics.

The feminists and gamers began shouting at one another. The feminists clamed that "ethics in gaming journalism" was merely coded speech for "all women should be raped by me while I'm playing video games, after which they should fix me a sandwich." They depicted the boys of GamerGate as a lonely agglomeration of unfuckable lads with tiny wee-wees.

In the end nothing was solved and everyone, on all sides, wound up more sexist than ever.

* * * * * * * * * * * *

#YesAllWomen

In May 2014, young half-breed Elliot Rodger fatally gunned down two women and five men, including himself. A self-proclaimed virgin—but not for a lack of trying—Rodger had left a rambling written manifesto and a skin-peelingly creepy video of himself vowing vengeance against two groups of people: 1) the women who refused to fuck him; and 2) the men these women chose to fuck instead.

Despite the fact that he killed more men than women, women of course turned his rampage into strictly a women's issue. After Rodger's killing spree when someone started the hashtag #NotAllMen to explain that very few men were woman-hating spree killers, a woman countered with #YesAllWomen, which essentially meant, "Yeah, well, OK, *technically* not all men are rapist psychopaths, but ALL WOMEN have to worry EVERY DAY about being raped and killed by one of you fellas who *is* a serial butcher of female bodies."

Can all women be annoying? Yes.

* * * * * * * * * * * *

#JeSuisCharlie

Twelve people died in January 2015 when our spiritual brethren who practice the beautiful religion of Islam shot up the offices of French satirical paper *Charlie Hebdo*. While the blood was still drying, hashtags such as #JeSuisCharlie and #IAmCharlie became some of the most popular Twitter hashtags ever. Across the planet, people who, if you want to get technical, actually *weren't* Charlie were expressing their phony solidarity by pretending to be the recently deceased staff members of a French newspaper.

One thing is for sure: Except for all of us who aren't Charlie, we are all Charlie.

* * * * * * * * * * * *

#OscarsSoWhite

Who runs Hollywood? According to Twitter, white people do. Even though black actors receive Academy Awards in numbers slightly higher than their quotient of the population, this did not impede black activists—who, as a rule, actively insist on being black during all of their activities—from screaming about racial injustice and lynchings and slavery and police brutality merely because no black actors were nominated last year. As partial penance, the "white" people who run Hollywood allowed the organ grinder's assistant of a comedian named Chris Rock to host the 2016 Oscars and make it one ceaseless carnival of white-bashing in the name of anti-racism.

* * * * * * * * * * * *

#BoycottClippers

Octogenarian Hebraic billionaire and NBA basketball team owner Donald Sterling became America's most hated man in 2014 when his mixed-race mistress released audio snippets of him begging her to quit bringing black guys to home games of his LA Clippers. Taken in context, his comments are more those of a cuckold than a bigot—he tells her it's OK to sleep with black guys, just don't embarrass him by showing up in public with giant grinning Mandingo studs when you're pretending to be his mistress, OK? One even feels a smidge of pity for the sclerotic sports mogul. Even though a subsequent tape release showed his double-crossing mistress V. Stiviano making far more damning comments about blacks than Sterling did, he was forced to sell his team and must now hide from black people for the rest of his life.

* * * * * * * * * * * *

#ICantBreathe

Like Ferguson, MO's Michael Brown, Staten Island's Eric Garner became a posthumous celebrity after he died at the hands of police. As with Brown, Garner wouldn't have died if he hadn't aggressively resisted arrest. Garner had a rap sheet of over thirty arrests and was free on bail that fateful day when he tussled with police who tried to handcuff him for illegally selling loose cigarettes on the street.

During the altercation while police attempted a chokehold on his massively blubbery frame—Garner was said to be incapable of walking more than a block without having to stop and catch his breath—he reportedly told police "I can't breathe" eleven times.

It seems that if one couldn't truly breathe, one wouldn't be able to say "I can't breathe" eleven times. Ya feel me?

The legend spread that Garner was choked to death. He instead died of cardiac arrest in an ambulance headed for the hospital. He may not have died if he hadn't been placed in the chokehold. But if he wasn't morbidly obese and didn't have preexisting heart conditions...and, again, if he *hadn't resisted arrest*...he'd still be alive today.

Still, the untold legions of Twitter warlords who adopted the #ICantBreathe hashtag in Garner's honor had at least one thing in common with him—they were all breathing when they said it and are thus all liars.

* * * * * * * * * * * *

#RefugeesWelcome

Because our golden-skinned leader Barack Hussein Obama loves America, the White House launched the hashtag #RefugeesWelcome last November on its Facebook page in the wake of the Paris terror attacks that killed at least 130 people. According to an official White House statement:

> Even as we intensify our efforts in coordination with our partners to take out ISIL, we cannot turn our backs on those most threatened by the terrorist group.

In other words, "Merely because 130 people just got murdered in Paris by Islamic migrants, let's keep ourselves safe by inviting more Islamic migrants into our country." Sounds like a plan!

* * * * * * * * * * * *

#ShoutYourStatus

Our woman-loathing patriarchal culture shames modern females in many ways—by insulting their vaginas, by implying that their vaginas smell bad, by lying and saying that sometimes women can be irrationally emotional (especially during their monthly cycle!), by saying that women who wantonly get drunk and sleep with every guy they can dig their claws into are sluts, by trying to make girls feel bad if they eat too many doughnuts and wind up 100 pounds overweight, and especially if they are riddled with sexually transmitted diseases like a 90-year-old hooker in Rotterdam.

But since this is April, and as everyone knows, April is STD Awareness Month, in comes the hashtag #ShoutYourStatus to encourage women with STDs to proudly tell the world things such as "Hey, I have herpes lol" and "I just gave my boyfriend AIDS—holla!"

One of the hashtag's co-creators, a woman with the remarkable name of Britni de la Cretaz, says that having STDs currently can lead to discrimination and thus "should be destigmatized." She also says she used to be a raging alcoholic in order to "cope with the weight of living in a white supremacist cisheteropatriarchy." She has genital herpes and is proud as *hell* about it.

* * * * * * * * * * * *

#ShoutYourAbortion

The chronological and spiritual and comedic precursor to #ShoutYourStatus, this hashtag was conceived by the perpetually hectoring hamplanet Lindy West and two feminist allies.

According to Wikipedia:

An image of [hashtag co-creator] Kimberly Morrison's unshaved armpit with a tattoo that reads "fuck the patriarchy" was used as the logo for the Shout Your Abortion social media campaign.

The legacy left behind by #ShoutYourAbortion is that it encouraged young females who'd opted to murder their fetuses after spreading open their gummy thighs—and thereby permitting a man's sperm to fertilize their precious, life-giving eggs—to announce loudly and proudly to the world that they'd snuffed the small life that had naively and innocently begun sprouting in their stubbornly barren wombs.

31

What The Hell Do You Mean By "Social Justice," Anyway?

In the summer of 2016 in Milwaukee, a black cop shot and killed an armed black man. In response, throngs of howling blacks rioted, looted, committed arson, and >randomly attacked whites.

If that makes no sense to you, that's because you're not an idiot.

While the blood was still flowing and the cars were still burning and the white people were still being dragged from cars and beaten into tomato paste, multiple cognitively dissonant apologists for urban dysfunction trotted out a hoary 1967 quote from Martin Luther King, Jr.:

Social justice and progress are the absolute guarantors of riot prevention.

If I am making the correct inference from the Right Reverend Dead Dr. King's words, this riot would never had occurred if "social justice" had been achieved.

What the HELL does that mean?

As a congenitally and resolutely antisocial person, I have a vague grasp of what is meant by "social." To mangle a biblical quote, wherever two or more are gathered, that's where I'm not.

But as a pathologically logical person, I blanch at the vagueness of the word "justice." The more I hear it used and abused, the more it seems to be a dishonest synonym for "revenge."

None of the Milwaukee rioters was victimized by the shooting. According to reports, the victim had a long criminal history and was turning around to point an illegally acquired gun at the black cop when he was shot dead in his tracks.

Excuse me for having oodles of grey matter and almost no melanin, but I fail to see the injustice here. Was the cop expected to simply allow himself to be murdered in the service of some dimwitted mob's reptilian notions of "justice"? I'm not a mind reader, but I suspect his family would have considered that to be very unjust.

And that's the problem with the word "justice"—it is entirely subjective. It cannot be quantified. The world's finest engineers would be incapable of devising a machine that could measure injustice in specific increments.

Despite the fact that the term "social justice" has zero inherent meaning, it is not only fools that are fooled by it. It chaps my freckled hide to hear otherwise intelligent people wax on and on and frickin' ON about "social justice" with roughly the same intellectual precision as if they were yabbering about ghosts or astrology.

But we currently inhabit an upside-down, inside-out, parallel-universe world where people mistake the subjective for the objective. When rumpled socialist nebbish Bernie Sanders was asked last fall whether black lives matter or all lives matter, he shrugged as if irritated at even having to be asked: "Black lives mattuh," he said in his rusty Brooklyn accent as if it were a settled scientific fact.

But it's not a fact. It's an opinion. It can't be proved. And the modern state of public discourse is so emotionally juvenile and intellectually bereft, I am required to explain a concept that kindergarteners should be able to grasp.

As much as I don't want to crawl into the minds of the dunderheaded Milwaukee rioters, I suspect that they beat and burned and smashed and slashed due to some half-baked notion that all of their problems were due to "injustice" rather than, oh, the statistically high possibility that they never met their fathers. Pretending that you've been victimized by "injustice" must be a soothing balm for the wounded souls of congenital losers.

A highly troubling thing about the concept of "justice" is that I've never heard anyone so much as *attempt* to define exactly when it will be achieved to their satisfaction. Since "injustice" is indefinable, so is "justice." The quest for justice appears to be insatiable. Whoever gets a little bit always seems to want a little bit more. Despite how much they insist that "social justice" is a real goal, they keep moving the goalposts. The finish line always looms dimly over the horizon, and even though we've "come a long way," there is always more "work to do." No one has ever specified exactly when justice will have arrived and everyone can breathe easily without worrying that they'll be sucker-punched or have their house burned down due to some nonfunctional moron's unquenchable sense of personal grievance and barely concealed shame.

What's worse, justice appears to be a zero-sum game. It always seems to come at someone else's expense. Due to some dumb sense of righteous retribution for American slavery—which Asians had no part in—modern Asian students must surrender 450 SAT points to receive the same consideration as a black student for admission to Harvard.

In most cases, I suspect that black students would consider that to be socially just, while Asian students would deem it a grievous injustice. For the most part, social justice depends on whether you're throwing the punch or getting hit by it.

The oft-chanted mantra "No justice, no peace!" carries an implied threat. If you don't give us justice as we define it—and you don't even get a right to define it, because you've been designated as the perpetrator of injustice—we will burn your whole city down. That's probably why MLK posited an either/or selection between "social justice" and rioting.

It is no accident that the loudest proponents of "social justice" are either willing dupes or outright beneficiaries of unchecked government power. According to a 2006 statement by the United Nations Division for Social Policy:

> Social justice is not possible without strong and coherent redistributive policies conceived and implemented by public agencies.

Friedrich Hayek, who called social justice a "mirage," claimed that its end game was "a government with totalitarian powers."

In a dystopian nightmare fantasy, I imagine myself standing before a rabid crowd of social justice warriors, barking at the subliterate, brainwashed throngs through a megaphone:

"What do we want?"

JUSTICE!

"When do we want it?"

NOW!

"Exactly how would you measure 'justice'?"

[crickets]

"How much justice is enough?"

[crickets]

"So why don't you all get jobs, quit eating my taxes for breakfast, and shut the hell up?"

[rioting and looting commence]

32

The Social Justice Glossary

I've recently been made aware of a strange new tribe who are referred to by racists, bigots, homophobes, lesbiophobes, transphobes, and bestialityphobes as "Social Justice Warriors." I think they used to call themselves "liberals" until it became clear that they don't care much for liberty. Males and females in this tribe both tend to wear beards and gather in urban coastal areas, where they pay too much for apartments, water, coffee, and bean sprouts.

They speak a strange and exotic tongue unfamiliar to my ears. But they repeat certain terms so frequently, I feel as if I've begun to get a handle on they're driving at. To the best of my ability, I will try to decipher what these buzzwords mean.

ACTIVIST—A person who isn't actively performing activities at an actual job.

ANTI-RACIST—A person who makes everything about race.

APOLOGIST—Explainer.

BLAMING THE VICTIM—Daring to suggest that conflicts

between humans are often complicated and that it's therefore childishly naïve to believe that one person is always entirely guilty and the other is always entirely innocent.

BULLIES—People who must be bullied into silence.

CHOICE—The act of forcing people to pay for a woman's one-night stands.

CORPORATIONS—Malevolent yet generally non-coercive superorganisms that must be combated with a malevolent and entirely coercive superorganism known as government.

CRITICAL THINKING—The act of swallowing the laughably implausible tenets of blank-slate equality without asking a single question.

CULTURAL IMPERIALISM—An antiquated system that must be destroyed in order to pave the way for the newer, more global form of cultural imperialism.

CULTURAL OTHER—White heterosexual Christian males.

DEBUNKED/DISCREDITED—A topic or idea that we don't really want to address, because we haven't actually debunked or discredited it.

DISADVANTAGED—Dumb and unskilled.

DISENFRANCHISED—People who've received a free public education yet still can't spell "disenfranchised."

DIVERSITY—A magical incantation used to divert your attention from the fact that it is strikingly similar to the words "divide" and "division."

DOG WHISTLE—A high-pitched screech from the enemy that only progressives are able to hear. Lately this term has been deemed offensive to canines and should therefore be replaced with "coded speech" wherever possible.

ELITES—Wealthy people on the political right. This term is never used to describe wealthy people on the left who control much of the media, government, and academia.

EMPOWERED—Loud and annoying.

EQUALITY—A concept that nearly everyone believes but no one has bothered to prove.

EVOLUTION—An indisputably true biological process that stopped occurring roughly 100,000 years ago when everyone became equal. Christians are the only ones who don't believe it's real, and racists are the only ones who believe it didn't stop 100,000 years ago.

EXTREMIST—Someone whose beliefs make us extremely uncomfortable.

FAIRNESS—A political strategy requiring that winners be treated unfairly.

FALSE EQUIVALENCY—A real equivalency that suggests our beliefs are false.

FASCIST—One who must not be tolerated under any circumstances and should instead be either lynched, sent to a gas chamber, or stomped under our boots.

FAUX NEWS—A biased news channel that presents an alternative to our preferred version of biased and false news.

FIGHTING THE POWER—Allowing oneself to be used as the unwitting tool of global power elites.

FORWARD—The direction one moves when headed toward a cliff.

FLYOVER STATES—Where the bad people live.

GLOBAL VILLAGE—A concentration camp from which there is no escape.

GLOBAL WARMING—A fashion trend that replaced the global-cooling fashion trend of the 1970s.

GOVERNMENT AID—Money the government takes from taxpayers and then partially redistributes to non-taxpayers after taking a cut for itself.

GRASS-ROOTS—Elite-orchestrated protests that occur in places where there is usually no grass and plenty of cement.

GREEN—Naïve and inexperienced.

GUN NUT—Anyone who owns a gun yet doesn't belong to the group that actually commits the majority of American gun violence.

HATRED—Anything that we hate.

HERSTORY—The part of history that is usually ignored because not much really happened.

HETERONORMATIVE—Sexually normal.

HIERARCHICAL—Anything that posits there is true diversity among human individuals and groups when it comes to skills and intelligence.

HOMOPHOBE—Someone with a distaste for sex that involves feces and AIDS.

HONEST CONVERSATION ABOUT RACE—Condescending lecture about race.

INDIGENOUS—Anyone too stupid to figure out how to defend one's own land.

INSTITUTIONAL RACISM—A persistent hallucination of ubiquitous racism that is so deranged, anyone who experiences such hallucinations should be institutionalized.

ISLAMOPHOBE—Someone so terrified of Islamic retribution, they're afraid to say anything bad about Islam.

LEVELING THE PLAYING FIELD—Severely tilting the playing field to achieve unnaturally equal results.

LOOKISM—A term used by ugly people to explain why beautiful people won't fuck them.

LOW-INFORMATION VOTER—A voter who refuses to accept our brand of low information.

MARRIAGE EQUALITY—The act of pretending that two people of the same sex who can't produce children are equivalent to opposite-sex couples who can produce children.

MISOGYNIST—One who believes that women are human beings who are fully capable of intentionally harming others.

NEANDERTHAL—A term that became acceptable to apply to those of European ancestry shortly after it no longer became acceptable to refer to those of African ancestry as apes.

NEGATIVITY—Anything that negates our naïve worldview.

NONPROFIT—A tax-exempt organization that pays its staff members handsome salaries.

OBJECTIFICATION—The act of noticing that women possess an object called a vagina.

OCCUPIER—Someone who eagerly flouts the law and will eagerly threaten lawsuits if you challenge them.

OFFENSIVE—Things that hurt our feelings and thus make us go on the offensive, whether through litigation or mob action, in order to counter them.

ON THE WRONG SIDE OF HISTORY—Someone who actually understands history and thus can see where all this is going.

OPEN-MINDED—Someone whose mind is closed to anyone who questions modern culture and modern authoritarian structures.

OUT OF TOUCH—Unresponsive to our relentless propaganda.

PARANOID—Justifiably skeptical of human nature and the manmade power organisms through which it operates.

PATRIARCHY—The group who invents everything, does most of the work, fights the wars, is at a legal disadvantage in gender disputes, and dies younger.

PSEUDOSCIENCE—Actual science that makes us pseudocrazy.

PROGRESSIVE—Someone who sees no contradiction in using the almighty state's blunt force to help "Fight the Power."

PROGRESSIVE POLITICS—Politics that favor a government that is progressively intrusive.

PROGRESSIVISM—The idea that progress can only be achieved by transforming the First World into the Third World.

RACIST—A word used by anyone, white or not, who hates white people.

RACISM—A derogatory scare word to describe a natural tribal instinct that is currently forbidden to only one tribe.

RAPE CULTURE—A fantasy society dreamed of by women who fantasize about being raped.

REDNECK—A racial slur used to describe people we assume are always using racial slurs.

RIGHTS—Things we wish to take away from the political right.

SEX-POSITIVE—A term almost exclusively used by someone with whom you would positively never want to have sex.

SOCIAL CONSTRUCT—A term used frequently by people who have never constructed anything of social value.

SOCIAL CONTRACT—A nonexistent legal document that no one in society has ever signed yet which binds everyone under threat of force.

SOCIAL JUSTICE—A fairy-tale belief system positing that the winners are solely responsible for the losers' plight.

SOCIOPATH—A non-socialist.

STARTING A DIALOGUE—Starting a monologue.

SUSTAINABILITY—A term that applies strictly to agriculture and the environment and is never to be used in economic, demographic, or cultural contexts.

TOLERANCE—Ideological intolerance.

TRANSFORMATIVE—Something in the process of accelerated change, as in when a normal cell mutates into a cancer cell.

TRIVIALIZE—To weigh mitigating circumstances and/or place into a proper historical context.

TRUTH TO POWER—The act of speaking obvious untruths in a quest to gain political power.

UPRISING—A violent riot characterized by looting, arson, rape, murder, and random acts of cannibalism.

URBAN—Black.

WHITE—The color of evil.

WHITE PRIVILEGE—The honor of being constantly blamed for everything bad throughout world history.

WHITE SUPREMACIST—Any white person who isn't constantly apologizing for their skin color.

WORKING CLASS—A heroic tribe of simple-yet-noble people we've never met but have read about in books.

PART II: PARODY

33

I've Finally
Realized We Live In
A "Rape Culture"

I was eating my usual breakfast this morning—a bowl of Kellogg's Rape Flakes swimming in the breast milk of female sex slaves chained in a basement—when I came across yet another headline about how we supposedly live in a "rape culture."

Being a white male in severe denial of the privileges the patriarchy accords to me, I rolled my eyes. *We do NOT live in a rape culture,* I said to myself, obviously lying. *In fact, most people consider rape even worse than murder. Only child molestation is considered worse than raping an adult woman, and even that is a form of sexual assault. The only time it's not considered repugnant by society is when a man's getting raped in prison—in those cases, you mostly hear a laugh track instead of horrified gasps, even though statistics show it's more than twice as common as females getting raped. There is not ONE WISP of evidence over the past couple generations that **anyone** of prominence in our culture encourages rape, much less the entire fucking culture.*

What an ASSHOLE I am!

Then I turned on the TV, and there was yet another talk show where a bunch of knuckle-dragging cavemen were high-fiving each other while laughing about how it's "cool" and "hip" to rape chicks. This was punctuated with TV commercials about how Cialis allows elderly men to rape women with confidence and how once you get her to guzzle about a dozen Miller Lites, it's much easier to rape her.

I tried to push this out of my mind as I grabbed the keys to my 1999 Dodge Rape Van and headed to a local library named in honor of convicted rapist Tupac Shakur to do some research. Even though I tried hard to look the other way, aisle after aisle featured books that either instructed young males how to rape women or celebrated great historical rapists and incidents of mass rape such as the Rape of Nanking by Japanese forces and the two million or so German women raped by conquering Soviet soldiers at the end of World War II. I searched and searched for hours, and I could not find one line in even one book that said rape is bad.

Flustered, I drove to a local college and snuck into a Women's Studies class. The male teacher was using a large pink phallic pointer on a female anatomical chart to illustrate the easiest and most effective ways to commit sexual assault against a woman.

Growing increasingly uncomfortable, I visited a local bar, only to see what I usually saw whenever I went there—a gang of men, including the bartender and the bouncer, were raping a young woman on a pool table. I turned away and quickly left.

As I motored home along Georgia Route 69—also known as the "Gang Rape Freeway"—I turned on the radio, only to hear that famous song by Journey. You know the one—"Don't Stop Rapin'."

Then it hit me with the blunt-trauma force of an unlubricated fist up my ass—we *do* live in a rape culture. There's no denying it. *All* the evidence proves it.

I only have two words to say: I'm sorry. I was wrong. OK—*five* words. But I think you get the point.

34

Calling Someone A "Douchebag" Is Hate Speech

Comrades, allies, and fellow travelers, at some point the question needs to be asked: At what point does calling someone a "douchebag" become hate speech?

As everyone knows, hate speech isn't free speech, and it isn't protected by the First Amendment. There is a line between free speech and hate speech. It's a real line. It is objectively and scientifically real. It's even on a map. You can look it up!

Maybe you should read a book sometime and shut your fucking privileged mouth, and then you'd realize that a little book called THE U.S. FUCKING CONSTITUTION makes no mention of the word "douchebag." Look it up! Just as the Founding Fathers couldn't have anticipated that you'd be able to buy baby-killing machine guns at Walmart, they had no idea that in the 21st century, people would be maligning cisgendered males by calling them "douchebags." I'm also pretty sure that none of the

Founding *Mothers* ever called any of the Founding Fathers a "douchebag," either. This is a simple FACT. Deal with it. Period. Case closed. End of discussion. End of story. It's even the end of the discussion you have after reading the fucking story.

What the Constitution *does* protect, however, is the right of everyone, no matter how absurdly sensitive or mentally unstable or generally annoying, to have their feelings protected as if everyone was a baby bird shivering in a cold nest on a frosty winter's morn. It grants the US government the right to seize someone's person and property and throw them in jail for life if they make someone cry. Again—read the fucking Constitution, you stupid lowlife pieces of shit who deserve to die.

We are a society. We are one. We live as one. We breathe as one. We think as one. And if someone isn't one of us, they obviously deserve to be exterminated. If someone somewhere says something that hurts somebody's feelings, it's only logical to think that if they aren't immediately thrown in jail, they will think it's OK to say hateful things and then start killing people. We, as a society, should not tolerate such intolerance.

You call these so-called "douchebags" primitive knuckle-draggers who are on the wrong side of history. Don't you realize that's EXACTLY what the racist purveyors of Manifest Destiny said about the bold and noble Native Americans as they were slaughtering them?

Do you realize how sexist the word "douchebag" is? Don't you realize that the douche was designed ages ago by indigenous European tribesmen as a cleansing feminine product engineered to make a woman's lady parts smell less offensive than they naturally are? How fucking dare you culturally appropriate a word designed and meant to improve women and apply it to men? If you're able to even look at yourself in the mirror without cutting your head off, I suppose that's because you're a sociopath.

Do you realize how racist the word "douchebag" is? I've *never* heard a Strong Black Man called a douchebag. Why? Do you hate black men? Are you trying to tell me they don't talk about women in demeaning ways, wear cheap cologne, and bond with one another in what should be openly mocked as a homoerotic manner? Why are you excluding them from this all-white country club? Racist much?

Do you realize how homophobic the word "douchebag" is? If you'd open your fucking eyes and think critically for a moment, you might notice that our media and Twitter never refer to gay men, lesbos, and the transgendered as "douchebags." Coincidence? Exclusionary much?

Do you realize how Islamophobic the word "douchebag" is? Muslim men can be merrily raping and torturing and beheading women. They can be stoning gay men to death. They can wear cheap cologne and sail across the Riviera bare-chested while hooting at the ladies, yet I've never heard one of you afford them the luxury of being called a "douchebag."

The word "douchebag" is also anti-Semitic, for obvious reasons.

As a cisgendered white male, I am an ally of the untold millions of American males who don't speak with a lisp or wear girl jeans or collect *Star Wars* memorabilia or like Robin Williams, and I have had fucking ENOUGH of the hate and the persecution and the dehumanizing speech that is casually tossed our way as if there was something "OK" and "acceptable" about it.

Y'alls need to STOP maligning the natural wonder drug known as testosterone and fearing it with a *Reefer Madness* level of absurd paranoia. This wonderful hormone enables men to be enticed by women's bodies at some point during puberty, whereupon they impregnate the woman, which leads to the miracle which we all know as "life." Without testosterone, y'alls wouldn't be here. Bow down.

Go ahead, I fucking DARE you: Tell me you don't feel pure HATE when you call someone a douchebag or when you call them a "piece of shit" who "needs to die." You are obviously seething with so much hate, you could fill Oprah Winfrey's vagina with it. You think your motivation is "justice." It is not. It's hate. That's a FACT. Read a book. Look it up.

So again, I must ask: At what point does calling someone a "douchebag" become hate speech? The question answers itself: At the very utterance of the word "douchebag." So don't say it, or we'll post your home address online and encourage people to kill you.

35

5 Ways To Convert Your Guy Friends Into Feminist Allies

Being a guy feminist isn't easy, especially when you spend a lot of time around guys who aren't feminists—and as the joke goes, the more time you spend with guys who aren't feminists, the more you realize why all women hate guys.

Take my friend "Joe," for example. His name may not really be "Joe," but to avoid potential lawsuits, let's call him "Joe." He's a good guy at heart and I've known Joe since high school, but he's so sexist, it makes me want to shame him in front of his whole family on Facebook.

Joe looks at women like a butcher looks at a hunk of meat. Women are not real to Joe the carnivore, Joe the predator, Joe the devourer, Joe the potential rapist. To Joe's sexist mind, women don't have souls, only holes.

Joe's brain has been sculpted to hate women, their vaginas in particular—ironically, the same vaginas from which all male sexists are spat forth as they enter this man's world—by an undeniably patriarchal media/legal/educational complex that clearly needs to be dismantled.

Whenever you mention your recent conversion to male feminism, Joe scoffs and says it's because Cindy dumped you for a guy who drives a motorcycle, but you tell him that every life experience, especially with women, is a learning experience, and that if you'd only been nicer to Cindy and converted to male feminism like she'd been urging you, she wouldn't have fallen for the "bad boy" and had that whole meltdown where she started acting like she really wasn't a feminist after all.

You've always thought that Joe was gross and creepy, but since you've decided to devote your life to becoming (never fully "being"—it's a perpetual process of *becoming*) a feminist ally, he seems grosser and creepier than ever, and you want to share important information with him about women that will make him a better man just for hearing it.

This is a handy and very effective five-point plan for converting sexist men to male feminism through a delicate balance of common sense and shaming.

1. Tell Him To Stop Making Sexist Comments

If Joe makes a sexist comment and there are no women around, say, "Joe, I think that was a sexist comment." If there are women around, say, "Joe, I *really* think that was a sexist comment." If he continues to make sexist comments, keep telling him to stop until he stops.

2. Tell Him It's Improper To Make Lewd Suggestions To Friends' Significant Others

Joe thinks you're "uptight" and "have a stick up your ass" and "need to chill out and have a drink" if you aren't constantly making rude, degrading comments about the anatomy of every female in sight. What Joe doesn't realize is that, in a very real way, *he is a rapist*. He rapes the "safe space" that should be left undisturbed inside every woman's head. You must be stern with him, but do it while offering the hope of redemption: "Joe, I don't think the way you're speaking about Bob's wife's ass is very respectful to any of us, yourself included."

3. Tell Him That Women Really Wouldn't Even Fuck Him If He Spoke Respectfully Toward Them

Joe's always talking about how all "bitches" are "sluts" and are "asking for it" and "really want it" and "like doing it a lot." If Joe were a lot more attractive than he is, such comments would be forgivable—in many cases, perhaps even charming. But what makes Joe's comments so disgusting is the fact that Joe is physically repulsive and doesn't even realize it. Once you convince Joe that his "issues" with women stem from a lifetime of being rejected by them because he is not a desirable mate, you will break his will and thereby prepare him to become a dedicated and militant male feminist until the day he dies.

4. Tell Him To Stop Laughing At Rape Jokes

Although most men will deny it, they all tell rape jokes and laugh at them when there are no women around. Tell Joe there's nothing funny about rape, there will never be anything funny about rape EVER, and that any man who laughs at rape jokes should be forcibly sodomized by a trained team of a dozen very muscular men. (Come to think of it, the idea of guys getting raped *is* kinda funny.)

5. Tell Him That His Opinions End Where Everyone Else's Feelings Begin

Joe probably whines a lot about "censorship" and "free speech" and "the First Amendment" and "the Constitution," but basically he's a baby who hides his fear behind tough but empty words. And if the little baby boy keeps running his mouth, if he keeps shooting those poison darts that he calls "words" at people, sooner or later someone will get hurt. And if someone gets hurt, then Joe will go to jail. And if Joe gets hurt in jail, that's the price of free speech. Free speech is not hate speech. Sorry, I think it's the other way around—hate speech is not free speech. Yeah. That's it. Tell Joe that it's fine if he wants to have an opinion, but you will get him jailed unless he keeps it to himself.

36

8 Forgotten Otherkin

I was cruising Tumblr as I am wont to do because I have tremendous empathy for insane white late-capitalism American teenagers on psychiatric medication who are in many ways the most spoiled crop of human beings ever to live but somehow feel guilty rather than thankful for it and thus suffer from "trauma envy" and constantly need to invent ways to feel oppressed.

The "otherkin" community, for you bigoted racist redneck Republican assholes who aren't tolerant and really need to be exterminated and might not be familiar with the term, consists of a rainbow array of people who insist they are not really human beings but due to unforeseen biological circumstances and botched cosmic coincidences happened to wind up hopelessly trapped in human bodies.

In case you're some blind privileged asshole and are unaware of this bold and brave community, here is a helpful list—a cleverly titled "kincyclopedia"—of some of the more popular breeds of kinfolk that includes alienkin, birdkin, dogkin, and wormkin.

If you have even one drop of empathy in your whole fucking rancid bigoted body, you might be able to relate to the plight of some hapless 14-year-old in Kansas who suffers the slings and arrows of living life as an earthworm trapped in a human body. Or maybe not. Maybe you're just that fucking *sick in the head* that you don't realize these people speak the truth and deserve not only empathy, but ample government funding. If that's the case, I hope a whalekin finds you and sits on you, squashing you to death for being intolerant of those who are different.

But as I was perusing that kincyclopedia, tears streaming down my cheeks because I am loving and empathetic enough to realize that these people suffer not from mental delusions but from the intolerance of FUCKING ASSHOLES who just can't accept that some people are in reality bicycles trapped in cages made of human flesh, I realized that even this list, as forward-thinking as it is, was not as "inclusive" as it pretended to be. Intersectionality is one of the most problematic junctions of the progressive community—I mean, it's like if you're standing right in the middle of the street trying to direct traffic where 100 roads converge, sooner or later you're going to get flattened by a garbage truck, right? I started screaming at my computer screen because this list neglected, probably on purpose, to mention some of the more alienated and marginalized members of otherkindom.

That's why I'm here to help. In our tireless quest to corral those who are different from us into one big community where in reality nobody thinks differently than anybody else for fear of perpetual ostracism and group shaming, we often exclude those who are so different that even those who are tremendously different don't want to touch them.

Here are eight types of otherkin that often escape notice because everyone's too busy patting dragonkin and dolphinkin on the back:

1. Turdkin

These are people—OK, not really *people*, but I don't want to get into some whole anti-ableist semantic digression—who outwardly appear to be human but are in fact giant bowel movements.

2. Normalkin

They might *superficially* seem weird—say, they're too skinny or their noses are too big or they have so much acne you think that their faces are eventually going to fall off—but they are in fact completely well-adjusted cheerleaders and jocks who inwardly shriek in pain because the world doesn't realize how normal and average they are.

3. Pumpkin

To the naked eye they appear "human," but in scientific reality they are gasoline pumps and thus favor PIV heterosexual intercourse. (In some circles they are referred to as "nozzlekin.")

4. Napkinkin

Existing on the societal fringes, they only seek to help others by wiping their lips and fingers after meals even without being asked to do so, only to be taunted and beaten and charged with sexual harassment.

5. Housekin

They suffer housing discrimination and thus chronic homelessness because our society refuses to develop housing large enough to house a house.

6. Nazi Kinheads

Mostly comprised of Jews, Gypsies, homosexuals, and Polacks, this group attempts to ingratiate themselves with the remaining dozen or so Nazi skinheads who still exist in the United States, only to find themselves rejected yet again. They cry a lot.

7. Merkin

Imagine the pain and shame of being a pubic wig that suffers scorn and bullying in a world that is prejudiced against the perfectly natural female human bush. Can you imagine that? No? Of course you can't. That's because *you're an asshole*.

8. Mexikin

These are "white" kids from flyover country who phenotypically appear to be "white" human beings but are in fact undocumented Mexican immigrants simply looking for a better life in America. There was a tragic 2005 incident in which a self-identified Mexikin attempted to join a cholo gang in East Los Angeles and lost his life in a hail of gunfire.

37

The 10 Most Microscopic Microaggressions Of All Time

This brief overview of *actual online words* that have *actually been published online* is a shocking example that hate is still the pillar of our society. Let us knock this pillar down and celebrate among the rubble. Here are ten real-life personal testimonials that are so heartbreaking, you'll want to pluck out your eyeballs and eat them:

1. I went into a McDonald's today to order a cheeseburger, and the clerk said, "How are you today, ma'am?" I can't fucking believe that in 2014, my genitals are still an issue with people.

2. I'm a strong, young, intelligent, empowered black female from the inner city. I went into a Gap store today to buy some jeans,

and the clerk, a white woman, came up with a smile and said, "How can I help you?" Obviously they thought I was going to steal something.

3. I'm a black police officer in a dangerous inner-city precinct. I was eating in the officers' lunchroom today, and a table full of white cops pulled out a chair and asked me if I'd like to join them. I could tell they were dying to call me "boy" but were too chicken-shit to try it.

4. I'm a 19-year-old white male who was brutally raped in broad daylight outside a Walgreens in Denver yesterday. The police came and took my story, then acted all "concerned" and called for an ambulance to take me to the hospital, where all the workers were very "kind" and "caring." Obviously they don't realize we still live in a patriarchy and that women get raped a lot more often. I'm so fucking sick of these false equivalencies.

5. I went out with some white friends and they didn't once mention I was black. I believe this is because they were afraid of being called racists, and if you're afraid of being called a racist, that's because you're obviously a racist.

6. I'm an intelligent single white female who got pissed at my boss yesterday because it was raining outside and he held the door for me as I was coming into the company. Does he think I'm too weak to open a fucking *door?!?* But this morning it was also raining outside and he didn't hold the door for me because I guess the asshole thinks I'm supposed to "take it like a man."

7. I have straight friends who never once ask me questions about being gay because obviously they hate gay people and don't want to think about what dicks taste like.

8. I went into a Walmart store and asked a worker there which way the restrooms were. He—of COURSE he was a white male—said,

"The men's room is that way." Yes, technically I'm a man, but I'm furious that he would feel entitled to gender me that way.

9. I'm a Latino who was riding the Chicago Transit Authority today. One white rider sitting across from me didn't make eye contact because obviously they're afraid of Mexicans. Another one looked straight in my eyes as if to say, "You don't belong here."

10. I'm black, and today I asked my sushi waitress what kind of soft drinks they serve. She said they only serve Coke. Obviously she thinks all black people do cocaine. She obviously also doesn't understand that in this society, most black people aren't able to afford regular cocaine. #SMH

38

8 Geometric Shapes You Didn't Realize Are Problematic

As anyone with two brain cells to rub together already knows, math is political, and this includes the Western imperialist social construct known as geometry.

The main problem with so-called "modern education" is that it still relies far too heavily on cruel patriarchal delusions such as "facts" and "logic," two discredited and debunked notions that have been demonstrated again and again to hurt the feelings of the oppressed and underprivileged. We, as a society, need math to be *inclusive*, and that naturally includes people who have problems with math.

This list is by no means intended to be comprehensive, but it should serve as a guide to all geometry teachers concerned with social justice that there are certain lines you should NOT cross while drawing lines on the blackboard.

1. Circles

Circles are potentially problematic because they are the shape of the planet Earth, and Republicans are standing in the way of not only a world without borders, they are also blocking comprehensive climate-change reform that would save the planet.

2. Rhombuses

The humble rhombus may look innocent, but in the minds of racists and imperialists, it is a dog-whistle—actually, a *shape-whistle*—that represents the "blood diamonds" which have torn apart sub-Saharan Africa.

3. Pentagons

This should be obvious to everyone who isn't a warmongering asshole, but the pentagon is actually a shape-whistle for a *pentagram*, the satanic symbol which secretly represents the so-called "Pentagon" building in Washington, DC, which is the seat of America's continuing wars of aggression as well as white males' collective sexual anxieties.

4. Parallelograms

Try saying "parallelogram" five times fast. Now, imagine that you have a speech impediment. The parallelogram is obviously so named in order to shame students with speech impediments from speaking up in class, therefore dooming them to career failure and lifelong loneliness.

5. Octagons

The eight-sided octagon in its most sinister form takes the shape of the seemingly benign "STOP" sign, which is yet another shape-whistle that the Tea Party uses to stop women, minorities, gays, and the crippled from making progress.

6. Ellipses

This egg-like geometric shape could be mistaken for either an ovary or a testicle, which may lead to confusion and subsequent derision. It is therefore innately transphobic.

7. Crescents

Americans who are on the wrong side of history—basically, all Americans who don't live in large cities and still cling bitterly to their Bibles and guns—are highly Islamophobic. Whenever they see a crescent, even if it isn't intentionally an Islamic one, they are prone to shoot.

8. Triangles

White supremacists and European colonialists are by nature historical revisionists who deny that their people lived in caves while Africa was a flourishing civilization with flying cars and highly advanced dentistry techniques. They don't like to acknowledge that the Egyptian pyramids were designed and built by black people.

We're all in this together, people, so please feel free to suggest your own problematic shapes in the comments. And if you don't think any of the shapes I listed here are problematic, you are obviously part of the problem.

39

I Told Myself To Stop Whitesplaining But Realized I Was Still Mansplaining

In my ongoing quest to make my very existence less problematic, I sat my pale ass down the other day to scold myself for the privileges that my lily-white skin affords me. As everyone knows, the only way to truly become a better person is to feel absolutely horrible about yourself.

I thought of all the women and the blacks and the Jews—*especially* the Jews—who are inconvenienced and "put out"—and I don't mean that in a sexual sense—by the cool DNA profile I received after spitting into a glass vial and sending $99 to 23andme.com:

James T Goad – 100% European

Northern European

72.1% British & Irish

3.9% French & German

0.1% Scandinavian

21.0% Nonspecific Northern European

Southern European

0.2% Italian

1.7% Nonspecific Southern European

<0.1% Ashkenazi

0.9% Nonspecific European

<0.1% South Asian

<0.1% Unassigned

I sat there flogging my soul as if it were a Kracker Kunta Kinte, blaming myself for inheriting the sins of my fathers because even though we all know that Christianity is bullshit, many of its concepts—such as intergenerational blood guilt—are useful if we truly want to live in a just, free, equal, progressive, happy, smiling, nice, sweet, nice, hate-free, nice, harmonious, nice society. Although I don't believe in the Judeo-Christo-Islamo God, I think even Neil deGrasse Tyson would agree that the cosmos invented skin cancer to punish white people.

Drenched in my salty tears, I thought of all those dogs biting black people in Alabama, all those firehoses that were sprayed on them—even though, to be frank, it gets very hot and muggy down South and the occasional firehose might actually be refreshing when you really think about it—all those burning crosses, all those Jews screaming as they were shoved into ovens as if they were Domino's Pizzas and not real human beings, all those black men swinging from trees (and I don't mean on swings!), and all those women who were forced to launder our underwear and sit at home knitting socks while we were selfishly being blasted to bits in coal-mining accidents and having our faces blown off on battlefields.

Seriously, it was the best self-inflicted guilt trip of my life. I was crying enough white tears to sell in a little vial on eBay for $15. I was hoping that I would finally become so demoralized that for the first time in my life, I would be a decent human being.

And then I realized who it was that was trying to make me feel guilty—a fucking MAN. My man side was guilt-tripping my white side, completely unaware that my man side was just as unfairly privileged as my white side.

Then my white side started yelling at my man side about female genital mutilation and Elliot Rodger and the kidnapped girls in Nigeria and how our sexist society makes Lena Dunham airbrush her pictures so she doesn't look fat and ugly.

My white side told my man side to divest itself of all its privileges, to which my man side replied, "I will, but only if you do it *first*."

Obviously, we—I mean "I"—was/were at a stalemate. Then, to make things even fucking worse, my heterosexual side decided to show up and start screaming at my white side *and* my man side about Stonewall and Matthew Shepard, and I realized I was in the middle of a full-blown Mexican Standoff. Even though I was trying to be good, I couldn't help whitesplaining and mansplaining and hetsplaining.

Clearly, I need someone else to explain things for me.

40

The US Postal Service Is Dominated By White Mails

I went to the Post Office to pick up my mail today, and every god-damned envelope was white. It was as if I'd fallen asleep and woke up in the fucking 1950s. I can't believe that we're even still *having* this discussion.

Sure, the US Postal Service employs plenty of Mailpersons of Color in a cynical attempt to temporarily deflect your attention from institutional racism, but—HELLO?—has everyone forgotten about slavery?!?! The Alamo? The Trail of Tears? The humble Coolies who built our railroads out West? Where are *their* envelopes?

Apart from the occasional manila envelope, when was the last time you received an envelope of color? Have you *ever* received a black envelope? A brown one? A red one? Nope. It's all white.

This is so fucked-up, it makes a man want to go full-blown bulimic.

Take a look in the mirror, America. You'll see a Klansman looking back in the form of a lily-white #10 envelope. And while we're on the subject, do you know why they're called "#10" envelopes? Because 10 times out of 10, the WHITE man gets the job.

It's like Newman—a *white* postal worker—told the all-white cast of *Seinfeld*: "When you control the mail, you control *information*." The information in this case is history, which was mostly written by dead white males when they were still alive. Time for us to rewrite history with a vibrant pack of multicultural crayons.

A journey of a thousand miles begins with one step. The US Postal Service's journey toward social justice will begin with one black envelope. Sure, we'll have to buy white-ink pens so you can see the address, which is problematic in itself, because it subverts the whole "multicultural crayon" narrative, but together we can make it work. Spread the news. Post this on Facebook. Write your Congresswoman. Tell your parents. Shame your friends.

And while we're at it, let's deconstruct the patriarchal notion that we *receive* "mail." Why must we submit and assume the receptive position as "mail" is delivered into our "boxes" and "slots"? Have you ever received "femail"? I think not! Instead of a "mailman" delivering your "mail," let's have "personpersons" delivering "person" to us in black envelopes. Then—and *only* then—will our society be halfway toward sanity.

41

Judge Orders Hitler To Undergo Therapy

PORTLAND, OR—Adolf Hitler is in trouble again. The infamous ex-dictator is no stranger to controversy, and last month in Multnomah County District Court, Hitler found himself under harsh media spotlights yet again when a judge ordered him to undergo anger-management counseling.

The shocking judicial decision came amid a routine probation-violation hearing that occurred after Hitler was found walking within 150 feet of a synagogue, a clear violation of his probation. Right before the judge issued his decree, Mr. Hitler, the Portland resident whom critics call The Most Evil Man in World History, erupted with a loud volley of invectives that had judge Ernest K. Jeske threatening to cite him for contempt of court.

* * * * * * * * * * * * *

"This is BULLSHIT!" Hitler had jumped up and screamed after the judge recommended he spend forty hours of community service cleaning racist graffiti off of synagogues and mosques in the greater Portland area, graffiti which many experts believe was left by Mr. Hitler himself. "I'm tired of you motherfuckers treating me like a goddamned STEPCHILD!" Hitler continued. "It's been more than fifty years since I killed a Jew, and STILL you're gonna put me through the wringer? FUCK that shit, man! Adolf Hitler ain't goin' *out* like that!"

"One more peep out of you, Mr. Hitler," Judge Jeske threatened, "and I'll have you taken out of here in handcuffs. Do you understand me, Mr. Hitler? In this courtroom, I'M *der Führer*."

Hitler smirked defiantly but remained silent as Judge Jeske continued.

"Mr. Hitler, I've just about lost patience with you," the judge said. "Our community's traditional method of correcting someone's behavior has been social disapproval and ostracism, but these things don't seem to work with you. Over the years, I've watched you float in and out of this courtroom over and over again, and I've never seen you exhibit the tiniest sliver of remorse for all the hurt you've caused others. You are one of the most selfish, self-absorbed characters I've ever run across. It's always Adolf, Adolf, Adolf. Therefore, you have left me no other choice but to recommend that you attend *Cage Your Rage*, which is a six-week anger-management class sponsored by the Oregon Department of Corrections. You'll attend six one-hour classes in a group setting where you'll hopefully get to the bottom of some of your anger issues and resentments. After you're done with the class, I want you to bring in your certificate, and we'll talk about dismissing this probation violation, OK? Now, do you have anything to say for yourself?"

"Your Honor," Hitler said, clearing his throat, "this really hurts my feelings. That's all. I feel very confused, and this really hurts my feelings."

"Mr. Hitler," the judge countered, "sometimes I wonder whether you *have* any feelings."

The judge also said that the name "Adolf" was perhaps a bit too harsh and was inextricably associated with Hitler's shameful past. "How about 'Todd' for a first name?" the judge suggested. "I would *trust* someone named Todd Hitler."

Regarding Hitler's being evil, the judge said, "Cut it out!" And on the topic of Hitler's legendary anti-Semitism, the judge warned, "Let me make this clear—if you kill any more Jews, it's straight back to jail with you."

* * * * * * * * * * * *

Outside the courtroom, Hitler appears shaken by the decision. "I've done some bad things, no doubt about it," he says, "but I think the judge is clearly overstepping the boundaries of fairness in this case. To me, this smacks of a personal vendetta. Just because of who I am—you know, I'm *Hitler*—people try to take advantage of me. It might have been fair if the judge asked for a public apology from me or something, but a *six-week* anger-management class? Ouch! How am I going to explain this at work?" Hitler says he'll attend the anger-management classes "only because I don't want to go back to jail."

Adolf Hitler became a Portland resident about twenty years ago after a more than forty-year stint in Argentina following WWII, a war that Hitler now wistfully calls "The One That Got Away." After moving here, he attracted immediate local attention when a *Willamette Week* reporter quoted him as saying, "The Jews run everything." The city's Jewish mayor, the Jewish head of the Chamber of Commerce, and the Jewish police chief all demanded that Mr. Hitler retract his statement. Instead of doing so, Hitler said that his detractors "need to chill."

"I was quoted out of context by that asshole from *Willamette Week*," Hitler now says. "I never technically said, 'The Jews run everything.' If you listen to the tape, you can *clearly* hear me saying something like, 'Boy, those Jews, they sure run a lot of stuff, y'know?' It was more like that. It was more innocent than it sounded.

"I'm not a Nazi anymore," Hitler tells me with a shrug. "The whole thing was just a big misunderstanding. I already apologized for the Holocaust. I mean, I felt really, *really* bad about it. What else do they want from me? I think I've learned from my mistakes, and I think I've grown as a person. Mostly, I really want to be left alone. And I think the Jews need to just *let it go*."

* * * * * * * * * * * *

The coffee pot isn't working again this week—for the third week in a row—causing some of the men to grumble when they enter the room for the meeting. The old wooden chairs squeak when you sit down in them.

The linoleum floors are scuffed and dull. The big wooden table in the middle of the room is covered in crude engravings, some of them unprintable, scratched in the wood by bored students.

This is where the angry men come to deal with their anger.

This is where Adolf Hitler is just another angry man among many.

"Adolf needs to stop hiding his feelings behind lofty notions about his race or his nation," says Cesar Sanchez, Hitler's anger-management facilitator. "He needs to think on a much smaller scale. He needs to stop worrying about Jews and Germans and start thinking about what's right for Adolf." Sanchez is an amiable, barrel-chested Chicano who served prison time after an armed robbery which left a Catholic nun permanently brain-damaged.

Hitler has been attending his anger-management classes for two weeks and "seems to be making progress," according to Sanchez. "He had a bit of an attitude when he first came in here," Sanchez remembers, "thinking he was all better than everybody and more famous than everybody and more supreme than everybody, but I took care of that quick. I got right in his face and yelled, 'Look, Hitler! I don't care if you're Mr. Big Bad Hitler! I ain't afraid of you, Hitler!' and I haven't had any problems with him since. Unlike a lot of these guys they send me, at least Hitler shows up for the meetings *on time* every week, and he's always very neatly dressed. Except for the fact that he singlehandedly started a World War which led to the deaths of fifty million people, he's really a model student. I wish *everyone* had his manners."

At this week's meeting, a fat, walleyed black man named Kelvis is talking about how his first love left him standing at the altar and how his life unraveled afterward. Kelvis begins crying as he recalls all the years wasted on crack cocaine, all the ruined friendships, and all the times police were summoned to his apartment to quell domestic disturbances with all the women he was using to try and fill his first love's place.

The room is silent except for Kelvis's sobs. Finally, Hitler reaches across the table and gently nudges a tissue box in front of Kelvis, who grabs a tissue and looks appreciatively at the former evil despot.

"Thanks, Hitler," Kelvis says in between the tears. "Man, I don't care what they say—you *all right!*"

After the meeting, Sanchez seems pleased with his client's progress. "Giving Kelvis the tissue box was the sort of thing you'd never expect from Adolf Hitler. But put him in a group filled with other angry men and tell him, 'Hey, Hitler, it's OK—*we hurt, too*,' and Hitler can finally relax, blow off some steam, and just be 'one of the guys.'"

Outside the meeting room, Hitler reflects on his compassionate act. "I saw that poor black man cry because he lost the woman he loved, and I felt compelled to help him. Why? Because I, too, once loved a woman and lost her. That woman's name was Deutschland."

* * * * * * * * * * * *

"Adolf's an absolute sweetheart, and I think that what the judge is making him do with these anger-management classes is *way* out of line." The girl making this statement is undoubtedly beautiful: platinum-blonde hair, a dolled-up face, full lips, fruitfully large breasts, and a look in her mascara-framed eyes that says she's ready for fun and mischief. But what's suspect is this twenty-one-year-old's romantic involvement not only with a man roughly ninety years her senior, but a man who would have most fathers loading a shotgun in order to keep their daughters away from him. She says her name is Spring and that she and Hitler have had a romantic relationship "for a full seven weeks now."

Spring claims she met Hitler at the Matador, a local bar said to be so filled with young, eager females that some have jokingly called it the Automatic Whore. "He walked into the bar with this buddy of his," Spring recalls, "and I don't know if you've ever seen Hitler enter a room, but it was *totally* impressive. I was like, 'Whoa—who's the hot old dude in the black suit?' Somebody told me it was Hitler and that a long time ago he almost ruled the world. It made me totally wet! I went over and introduced myself, and before you knew it, we were having sex out in back of the Fred Meyer's." Spring says that Hitler is a "fabulous lover" who is "wonderfully endowed" and shows "amazing stamina for a man his age." She also says she doesn't listen to all the friends who have become concerned for her safety since she hooked up with Hitler. "They say he's done a lot of bad things in the past, but so far Addy has been nothing but sweet to me. I love him madly, and after he finishes up with the final three weeks of that goddamned anger-management class, we plan to be wed."

* * * * * * * * * * * *

What does the future hold for Adolf Hitler? Will the admittedly draconian measure of forcing him to take a six-week anger-management class yield the desired results of a healthier, happier Hitler? We know that Mussolini responded well to Paxil and that one-on-one Jungian therapy is working wonders for Mahmoud Ahmadinejad. Will six grueling encounter sessions with other angry males be the ticket that pries open his heart like a clamshell and forces him to accept once and for all that he *is* a member of the master race—the *human* race?

Hitler seems to think so.

"I wake up in the morning," Hitler says, "and I throw open my bedroom shutters to see the birds all aflutter and the golden sun gently dusting the leaves on the trees, and I feel happy to be alive. I look back soberly on the mistakes of my past and say, 'Wow, dude, *I fucked up.* I fucked up *royally.*' But you know what? It's OK! God isn't done with me yet. Sure, people are probably always gonna give me a hard time for being Hitler, but I can accept that. Hitler's the one who has to live with Hitler, y'know? These days, especially after my three sessions of Mr. Sanchez's class, I can look at myself in the mirror while I'm shaving around that little mustache of mine and say, 'You're all right, kiddo. You're only human.' Imagine that! *Hitler's* only human. That was really hard for me to say, but it feels really good saying it."

42

White Man Blames Women, Nonwhites For His Problems

Auto mechanic Edgar Bison of Vernonia, Oregon, isn't your average racist. You might even call him an extra-special racist.

What separates Bison from the ordinary white racist...what pulls him ahead of the pack, if you will...is that he blames blacks and women not only for his general belief that America's culture is rapidly declining, but he also accuses them of causing his everyday personal maladies.

For instance, Bison suffered a toothache a few weeks ago that he blames on "radical Canadian bulldykes." And he has filed a personal lawsuit against feminist author Andrea Dworkin, blaming her for the fact that he is "still on the goddamned waiting list for a parking space in my condo building."

Bison also fingers women and blacks for causing seemingly unrelated global events. He insists that the World Trade Center terrorist attacks were orchestrated by the Crips street gang as vengeance "against White America" for rapper Tupac Shakur's murder. He claims that his favorite football team, the Buffalo Bills, have never won a Super Bowl due to "the scourge of interracial dating."

However repellent I find Edgar Bison as a human being—and, c'mon, people, he *is* a human being, despite the fact that he needs reeducation, forcibly if necessary—I'm intrigued by his mind. What sort of person would entertain such horrible thoughts in this day and age? My heart racing at the thought of forbidden, long-suppressed racial thrills, I called Bison at his auto-repair shop and tried to arrange an interview. After an initial rough patch in the conversation (he threatened to kill me if I turned out to be a black woman, and I assured him I wasn't), he agreed to a brief chat over donuts and coffee.

We try to speak over the hubbub of the lunchtime crowd at the Golden Puffball donut shop in the sleepy mountain town of Vernonia, Oregon. Although a kind man (he paid for the donuts), Edgar Bison radiates a vague sense of menace and desperation. His pores exude a reddish oily substance not unlike hippo sweat. His waxy dandruff flakes fall softly to the floor whenever he shakes his head or moves suddenly. And his face is so pinched, it almost appears to have been altered using Adobe Photoshop's new "Liquify" filter.

So, Edgar—exactly what classifies someone as a "nonwhite?" I ask him as I lick a hardened morsel of white donut cream from my denim jacket's wrist sleeve.

"That's easy," Bison replies. "They're nonwhites. They're the people who ain't white. They ain't got no white in 'em. And they're the ones who cause my problems. Them, and the women. I don't have a single problem I can't blame on blacks and women!"

I think you blame blacks and women in order to escape responsibility for your own problems and shortcomings, I boldly counter, proud of myself.

"But I *would* take responsibility for my problems," Bison retorts, "if blacks and women weren't responsible for them!"

TAWANI FULANI IS A BLACK WOMAN who moved to Vernonia with her family from South Carolina a little over a year ago. For nine months now, she's toiled as a parts clerk at the same auto shop where Bison works. He initially ignored her entirely (although she suspects he's the one who placed the "Urkel" doll in her locker only a week after she began working there), but she says now he's softened and will nod at her "every so often if he isn't in too bad a mood."

Fulani, an amiably freckled black woman, complicates matters: Not only does she refuse to accept blame for Bison's problems, she turns the tables and blames Edgar Bison for all of *her* problems.

"Edgar's a very sloppy employee," she notes as we dance the lambada at an interracial strip club/juice bar just south of Vernonia. "He never cleans up his mess in the lunchroom when he's done eating lunch there. There are wrappers and French fries and pickle slices all over the place. It's a big pain in the ass cleaning up after him. So he's wrong. I should be blaming white men like him, rather than the other way around. White men like him have been getting away with this sort of shit for five thousand years."

"How do you know it's been five thousand years?" I ask.

"I don't know," she shrugs. "I guess it sounded good."

43

Portland's White Community: Who Are They? Where Are They Going? What Do They Want From Us?

The Village Inn restaurant on Northeast Broadway is bustling with people on a typically blustery Portland winter afternoon. Latinos, Asians, and blacks mingle effortlessly. It could be any restaurant in any city in America.

And then a group of whites walks in.

All eyes turn toward them. The normal restaurant buzz turns immediately silent. It takes the soothing ministrations of Chandrita, the restaurant's charming Indian hostess, to escort the whites to a partially obscured table near the kitchen door, averting a possibly violent altercation. Once the whites are safely tucked away in the rear, the loud restaurant buzz resumes.

At one point, a black girl of four or five years old wanders over to the whites' table. She's wary but curious, as if spotting an unknown exotic breed of animal for the first time. She holds out her toy rubber ball for them to observe.

Again the restaurant is silent.

The white people smile. "That's a nice rubber ball," one of them says.

"Honey, get back here," the girl's mother yells, somewhat angrily. "Bring your ball back and leave those damn *white* people alone."

A few blacks titter. The smiles fade at the white table. The whites quietly don their jackets, pay their check, and leave.

* * * * * * * * * * * *

In a drafty warehouse across the river from downtown, Trudi Jensen applies blackface to her entire naked body while a handful of bored art-student types watches. "Do ya like me now? Do ya like me now? Do ya like me, NOW THAT I'M BLACK?!?" she chants, getting louder with each repetition. She then drinks an entire gallon of chocolate milk, defecates on stage, calls it her "baby," and launches into a soliloquy by Hattie McDaniel from *Gone With the Wind.*

A former highway flagger who has built a rabid cult following around her "Happy White Girl" character, performance artist Jensen calls Portland's whites "the invisible people." When a black boyfriend threatened to break up with her if she refused to get a hair weave, Jensen underwent a radical reclamation of her whiteness. She dumped him, shacked up with a white female partner, and began writing the basic outline for Happy White Girl. "It's hard enough being a woman in this world," Jensen tells me in her dressing room after the show, "but when you throw being white on top of that," she says, removing her blackface with a Noxzema-smeared cotton ball, "it's almost impossible to get by sometimes."

* * * * * * * * * * * *

"As a white guy, I might as well be a Martian in this town," Albert Scholls says in between bites of a "Big Rig" omelette at the Jubitz truck stop near the Washington border. "It's like, people look at you like they've never seen a white guy before." Scholls, who grew up in Canby but now lives in Portland, is riding high on the success of his first book, *White Men are From Mars, Black Men Got Big Penis*. A *New York Times* best-seller, *White Men* is a funny-yet-sharp deconstruction of stereotypes that white males suffer in modern-day America. "What I really hate," Scholls continues, "is when people want to be your friend just because you're white, and they think it's hip to have a white friend now. I have a lot of bitterness issues about being a white guy in this racist country. Imagine being a Martian, but you don't live on Mars, and that's what it feels like to be a white man in Portland sometimes. It's hard to maintain your anger sometimes. You just want to grab some of these people by the collar and say, 'LOOK, motherfucker, I may be white, but I'm a PERSON just like you!'"

* * * * * * * * * * * *

"We find it hard to hang out with other couples because we're white," Shannon Winston tells me as she sits inside her trailer near 82nd St., knitting her newborn son some footies. "When I met my fiancé Larry, it was like a godsend. Wow! Another white person! Somebody who understands what it's like to be white in Portland and what white people go through here." Winston met soon-to-be-husband Larry Kirby at a White Singles Dance in Southeast Portland. Such dancing events are sprouting up all over Portland's white ghettos as a response to the prejudices and pressures that white dancers sometimes face in Portland's interracial nightclubs. "I just hope my son can grow up in a world where it's safe to be a white boy," Winston tells me. "It'd be nice to live in a world where a white boy could go to a dance club where black boys are dancing without being afraid of getting hurt."

* * * * * * * * * * * *

Who are Portland's whites? here do they come from? What do they believe? And why are they so hated?

Most white people can trace their ancestry to "Europe," which is a continent on the other side of the Atlantic Ocean from us. A few hundred years ago, many white "Europeans" (the word for people who come from Europe) came over here and did a lot of bad things such as killing Indians and making black people pick cotton against their will.

Believe it or not, Portland used to be a predominantly white town. Back in the mid-1800s, whites outnumbered nonwhites by something like eight hundred and fifty billion to one. But whites, as notoriously wild and impossible to tame as they are, proved to be an unreliable labor pool. So Portland's land barons began encouraging a mass migration of nonwhites into the city, and whites have become Portland's Forgotten People ever since.

* * * * * * * * * * * *

"Some people don't think white people are people, but we're people, too," Rex Bitford tells me over a bowl of "macaroni and cheese," a popular white delicacy. Bitford is the rare white Portlander who has risen above his humble white roots and learned to, as he puts it, "use the system which has so sorely oppressed my people and make it help my people." Bitford receives a healthy yearly stipend to chair the White is a Color Foundation, a Portland think tank devoted to "helping white people speak out for our rights and get noticed." Bitford says that the Foundation is making progress in "helping white Portland lift itself up by the bootstraps and take pride in its Portlandy whiteness." He cites a recent study the Foundation financed which concluded that "if white Portlanders had it to do all over again, sixty-three percent of them would still be white." Every Christmas, Bitford hosts a Walking Tour of White Portland History which has proven popular with whites and nonwhites alike.

Bitford speaks about white issues at colleges and corporate seminars. He says that every crowd is initially skeptical but brightens up after he softens them with this joke:

Q: How many white people does it take to screw in a light bulb?
A: One. We're just like everybody else!

"We don't have a problem with any other race," Bitford says. "We're just happy we're white, that's all. White is often perceived as a non-color, an absence of color, when it's actually a rich, beautiful color—some would say the most beautiful of all. And white Portland is a vibrant community with a rich cultural tapestry."

"What do you mean by 'rich cultural tapestry?'" I ask him.

"You know," he stutters, "I mean that it has a *rich cultural tapestry* and stuff."

* * * * * * * * * * * *

"Back in Europe, their people are eating each other alive," says Amiri Abu-Jabubi, a conservative black nationalist and author of *I Did Yo Mama, White Boy—Now What?* [Black Tiger Books, 1999]. "I mean, let's tell the truth here. Europe is a primitive continent. It's not like we did a disservice to these white Europeans by bringing them over here, with our high standards of living. Maybe one of these days, these white crybabies will stop their sobbing and get to work on repairing the problems within their community, most of which are caused by the whites themselves. If white America wants to get its act together, it needs to drop the 'white' and focus on the 'America.'" Abu-Jabubi says that organizations such as the

White is a Color Foundation are insulting to "the honest whites who try to fit in and make an honest living."

* * * * * * * * * * * *

At a park in Northeast Portland, a large group of white people gathers together for a family-reunion picnic. (Until very recently, white Portlanders were forbidden to assemble in public.) White women serve hot dogs, peanut-butter sandwiches, and hard-boiled eggs dipped in mayonnaise. White men talk about ice hockey and auto racing. White children play with white toys such as the Hula-Hoop and the Hacky Sack.

"I'm proud to be white, but sometimes it hurts to be white," says Rutherford B. Hayes, a white Portlander who says he wants to move his family to another state because of Portland's racism. "A white man can't ask for the time of day in this town without a dozen cops and District Attorneys going for his throat," Hayes says, biting into a peanut-butter sandwich. "And they always think we want the black women. That's a big one—they all think that white guys want the black trophy girlfriend. I don't know about some of my white brothers, but I'm happy raising a white family with a beautiful white wife. I know that our mass culture, with the mass media and the mass culture, you know, preaches a standard of black female beauty, but I find white women the most beautiful of all." Hayes describes himself as a "racialist" rather than a "racist" but refuses to elaborate. "It wouldn't be fair to say I hate black people and other nonwhites," he says, "but I certainly *distrust* them. They're sneaky."

* * * * * * * * * * * *

All over Portland, white people are starting to be recognized for their accomplishments instead of their skin color. White Portland has seen some tough times, but it continues to search for acceptance in an often hostile world. We hope for the day when normal

Portlanders don't look at white people as white people, but as "just plain folks."

44

Life Is Unfair, And I'm Here To Change That

You should really count your blessings that you're safe, warm, and viewing this on a computer, because there are children in India right now who can't even afford toilet paper.

I realized a long time ago that life is unfair, and because this was clearly unacceptable to me, I made it my life's mission to change all that.

But maybe you're one of those "people" who don't have a problem with unfairness. If that's the case, I truly feel sorry for you.

All I ask is that you hold my hand—which, in truth, may be larger and more capable of inflicting damage than your hand, even though in the end, a hand is just a hand and your hand is no better than mine—and walk through this unfair world with me.

Right now a child is starving somewhere. A woman sits alone, crying. An old person just shit their pants but is too crippled to wipe themselves, and their state-provided healthcare worker won't be arriving for another four hours.

Are you OK with all that? Seriously? How the hell do you sleep? How do you look at yourself in the mirror? All I can say is that I'm glad I'm not you.

Bob Dylan—who *seriously* needed a good hair conditioner—once said, "He who is not busy born is busy dying." If you aren't part of the solution, you're part of the problem. And if you aren't with us, you're against us. Let us march together against everything that's wrong in the world. And if you don't march with us, don't be surprised if we step on your head along the way. If you want to make an omelette you have to crack a few eggs, and I plan to make enough omelettes to feed an entire homeless shelter.

45

Why the Fuck Are There No Gay Drivers In NASCAR?!?

I've been following Yahoo! Sports lately not because I like sports or am any good at them, but because they've been on the forefront of the righteous cultural battle to make everything around us gay.

They recently did a brave article about how the Minnesota Vikings fired a punter merely because he supported gay marriage. *ASSHOLES!*

They also did another recent article where Charles Barkley said that he played with gay players in the NBA. *THIS IS GOOD!!!!!!!!*

And there was another recent one about "young gay athletes." *THIS IS IMPORTANT!!!!!!!!!!!!!!!!*

Not to mention, although I'm now going to mention it, they did yet another recent one exposing hateful "anti-gay prejudices" in sports. *NOW WE'RE ON THE RIGHT TRACK!!!!!!!!!!!!!! SOCIAL JUSTICE, Y'ALL! WOO-HOO!!!!!*

By my last count, they also published nearly 75,000 articles about NBA player Jason Collins announcing that he's gay, gay, gay! *YAY! (!!!!!!!!!!!!!!!!!!!!!!!!!!!!!!!!!!)*

And last week I covered their brave and hard-hitting exposé about the fact that while the gays may be making advances into the sporting world, sexism is still a HUGE problem. *BRAVO! KUDOS! HATS OFF! TRUTH TO POWER!!!!*

Clearly the most important issue currently facing the sports world is whether there are enough gay people in it. All you homophobes may disagree, but that's predictable, but I must warn you: Time is not on your side, and you are dying as I type this. Oops! One just died before I finished that last sentence. *LOL!!!!!!!!!!!*

Pushing and shoving and cramming and thrusting the gays-in-sports issue even further into the notoriously homophobic, Southern, Republican, Neanderthal, sweaty, fat, ugly, and dysgenic world of stock-car racing, Yahoo! boldly went where no *Homo sapiens* has gone before to ask a simple-yet-crucial question: WHY THE FUCK ARE THERE NO GAY DRIVERS IN NASCAR?!?

Now, I don't consider motor racing to be a sport, but that doesn't mean it shouldn't be filled with gay people, anyway. The issue here is justice. And leveling the playing field—or, in this case, the racing track. We need to look forward rather than backward. We need to stamp out bigotry and hatred wherever it exists. Down with the hate! Death to the haters! Kill the haters! Form giant mobs to beat the haters to death! *NO MORE H8!!*

46

Why Don't They Just Be Honest And Call It "Rapebook"?

"Dear" Mark Zuckerberg:

What are you—some kind of rapist or something?!?!

Unless you answer this Open Letter, I'm going to have to conclude that you ARE a rapist, because if you aren't, why the FUCK(!) would you tolerate a page called "Horrifying Pictures Showing Violence Against Women" on your website, dude?

Really?

Seriously?

W...

T...

F??

A woman gets raped every nine minutes in the UK. How can you, with all your trillions of dollars, possibly know how painful and exhausting it is for that woman?

It says that you eagerly host pictures of women with their vaginas ripped out and eaten; women with their clitorises sawed off and used for costume jewelry; women with aluminum baseball bats inserted all the way up into their vaginas; underage girls dressed in provocative underwear; elderly women forced to blow entire minor-league baseball teams; college girls being treated as rape piñatas by laughing asshole jocks with suntan lotion on their noses; white men under-tipping black waitresses; women being run over with tanks and then forced to give handjobs to the tank driver; and women having everything but their vaginas cut off and fed to wolves.

And this is "COOL" with you?

I have one word for you: FUCK YOU!!!!!!!!!!!!

Sorry—TWO words.

We must NOT TOLERATE THIS. We must stand together. After we've assembled and are standing together, we must march together. As we are marching together, we must decide on a destination. There is NO other way.

Call your Congressperson. Inform your parents. Talk to people on the bus, even if they don't want to listen to you.

This is unacceptable.

If you need it spelled out, it's u-n-a-c-c-e-p-t-a-b-l-e.

Facebook is a place where people should meet and share progressive ideas. It is NOT a place for our eyes and souls to be relentlessly cyberraped.

Fuck you, Mr. Fuckerberg. Fuck you in the ass with a pair of studded nunchucks. And I hope it hurts. I hope you scream. I hope it gets filmed.

47

Fabricated Hate Crimes By The Transgendered Are Still OK!!!

Transgender people still face EXTREME FUCKING PREJU-DICE by stupid fucked-UP RACIST WHITE REDNECK ASS-HOLES merely because they mutilate the FAKE BODIES nature has given them so that it coincides with the REAL gender identi-ties that REALLY EXIST inside their heads! ??How many FUCK-ING TIMES do I have to explain this, you ASS-HOLES?!?!?!!?!?!?!?!?!?!?!

Anywayz, a transgender teen in a California town with the SICK cisgender macho name of "Hercules" recently reported they were beaten up by TRANSPHOBIC DICKHEADS, and even though the story wasn't TRUE AT ALL, it has an important lesson for all of us.

In the face of the HATEFUL backlash that occurred when the

story was revealed to be totally fake, a wise woman stepped in and said the following:

"There is still an important piece of the story, which is that trans youth do face elevated levels of bullying and violence, including physical assaults at school," said Carolyn Laub, executive director of the Gay-Straight Alliance Network. "Even if this particular story isn't true, the school's response, to put in place plans for bringing the community together and addressing school safety and climate, is a good outcome."

So THERE! Fuck the transphobic! They're ABNORMAL! GOD, I could kill someone today. Time to take my meds and hormone pills. I'm Audi. FUCK you!!!!!!!!!

48

Sexual Justice Is
Never Pleasant

Toru Hashimoto is the loudmouthed mayor of Osaka, Japan and should really have his balls cut off and fed to him with chopsticks after what he just said about Japanese troops' forced use of an estimated 200,000 "comfort women" as undernourished, uncompensated, underappreciated, and overly smelly prostitutes during World War II.

Inspired by Western capitalism and colonialism, Japan, spurred on by its patriarchal emperor, decided it'd be cool to just stomp across China and parts of some place called Korea during that war, using women as sperm spittoons to satisfy the insane and always sadistic male sex drive.

But according to Hashimoto—get this—there was NOTHING WRONG WITH THAT:

> *"Anyone can understand that the system of comfort women was necessary to provide respite for high-strung, rough and tumble crowd of men risking their lives under a storm of bullets."*

Rrrrrright. And I guess when a soldier who's pillaging, killing and raping needs to take the "edge" off, brah, he just holds a woman down and sprays her with a storm of sperm, right? Nothing wrong with that, right? It's not like women have been through enough, right? What an ASSHOLE!!!!!!!!!!!!!!!!!!!!!!!!!!!!!

If you see a Japanese person in the street today, ask them why they did it. More importantly, ask them what they're going to *do* about it. Don't let up on them until they either run away or call the cops. We're talking about sexual justice here, and justice is never pleasant.

49

The World's Most Racist Cereal

Racist assholes recently went on YouTube to spread open their filthy ass cheeks, open up their racist assholes wide, and shit all over what seemed like a nice, friendly, non-racist Cheerios commercial.

The commercial, which should be applauded, celebrated, and shown in EVERY SCHOOL ACROSS THE COUNTRY, features an absolutely adorable young mulatto child spawned by a white woman and a black man—the only proper interracial combination with which to smash the dominant white-male patriarchy.

Of course, these RACIST FUCKING ASSHOLES couldn't stand the idea of a huge, throbbing, veiny, thick, delicious, rhino-sized black cock ramming into that fair white maiden's so-called "sacred" vagina, so they started leaving comments to the effect of, "This is wrong," "This sucks," "She's a mudshark," "Who would fuck that big baboon?," "I'll kill that coal-burner the moment I get the chance," and things so unbelievably racist, I won't reprint them here because I don't want to start crying again.

FUCK THOSE RACIST ASSHOLES!!!!!!!!!!!!!!!! is all I can say about that. FUCK them. Really. FUCK them.

But then I started thinking—have you ever eaten Cheerios? Have you ever looked at an individual Cheerio? What about a group of collective Cheerios? Notice the color?

That's right—they're *ALL WHITE!!!!!!!!!!!!!!!!* We're not talking about Count Chocula or Cocoa Puffs here! We're talking about a breakfast cereal that excludes Grains of Color.

I also noticed another thing—what do people usually put on their Cheerios? *Milk!* WHITE milk!!!!!!!!!!!!! I'd estimate that they use chocolate milk in maybe 3% of the cases, if that. Chocolate milk is unjustly underrepresented in the national milk industry.

So what we're dealing with is an all-white breakfast cereal that is bathed in all-white milk 97% of the time. Are you OK with that?!?

WHERE'S THE OUTRAGE?!?!?!?!?!?!?!?!

I say we, as a multiracial society, should ~~boycott~~ girlcott Cheerios and all products by General Mills, whom I'm sure is some rich old WHITE GUY, because they ALL are. What kind of General *was* he, anyway? Probably not the kind who fought and died in the trenches like brave Men of Color did.

Fuck this! Fuck it where it breathes! I'm so mad, I could eat my own tongue.

50

This White Supremacist Fried Chicken Restaurant In Thailand Is Clearly Unacceptable

What the FUUUCCCCKKK?????????????????????

As much as I try to stamp out racism wherever I find it—which is EVERYWHERE—one person can only do so much to right historical wrongs and to set this world on a path toward global harmony and social justice.

But I can't be everywhere at once, and that includes Thailand.

Some FUCKING ASSHOLES in Thailand internalized the rotten tenets of white-supremacist colonialism and thought it'd be a "cute" and "hip" and "ironic" and "funny" idea to open a fried-chicken restaurant called "Hitler."

As I said before: **What the** *FUUUUCCCCKKK?????????*

Everyone involved with this restaurant, including not only the founders, but all the workers, everyone who's ever eaten there, and any ASSHOLE American tourists who thought it was "funny," needs to be KILLED.

Not once, but TWICE. Kill them, bury them, dig them up, and then kill them again. But don't do it quickly. Make them suffer.

Kentucky Fried Chicken, which originated in the RACIST state of Kentucky and was founded by a RACIST asshole named Colonel Sanders, is threatening to sue the "Hitler" restaurant for defaming its name, but I call BULLSHIT!

Are you seriously trying to tell me that some neo-Confederates have the moral standing to call out neo-Nazis on racism? Really? Seriously? *ARE YOU FUCKING KIDDING ME!?!?!?!?!?!!?!?!?!!?!?!?!?!?!!*

You're ALL racists, and I'm calling you ALL out! Name the time and place, and I'll be there. I will FUCK YOU UP!!!!!!!!!!

The only ones who aren't racists in this story are the chickens. No, they are more like tiny Jews being led to slaughter in the name of an INSANE AND BLOODTHIRSTY DICTATOR.

FUCK you, Adolf Hitler, you one-balled pro-corporatist white-supremacist anti-Semitic Randian sociopathic psychopath. It's about time someone took a stand and finally said it:

Hitler is NOT COOL.

And if you disagree, it's off to the ovens with you!!!!!!!!!!!!!!!!!!!!!!!!!!!!!!!!!!!!!!!

51

They're Already Misgendering The Royal Baby

Everyone with TWO FUCKING BRAIN CELLS to rub together knows that we live in an evil world ruled by racist white supremacists who constantly fantasize about raping women and peeing on homosexuals.

And this is why we FIGHT. This needs to be CHANGED—like, fucking NOW.

England isn't as bad as Germany, which next to the American South is the most disgusting and EVIL fucking country ever to disgrace this planet, but it's still really fucking BAD, especially since it still clings to antiquated, debunked, discredited, and pseudo-scientific notions such as sexual dimorphism, nationhood, and soccer.

This became FLAMINGLY clear yesterday when the new

"Royal Baby" was born and the only thing anyone wanted to know was, "Well, duh, what kind of GENITALS does it have?"

There's a name for that kind of thinking. It's called *CHILD PORNOGRAPHY!!!!!!!!!!!!!*

All across the right-wing media spread this obvious lie: "IT'S A BOY!"

Listen up, you patriarchal, cisgendered, slave-raping, tobacco-chewing ASSHOLES: It may have a PENIS, but it, and IT ALONE, gets to decide whether it's a boy or a girl or any of the 32 flavors in between.

That's so fucking obvious. It's right before their eyes, yet they can't see it. England, you're almost as SHITTY as America. Not quite, but almost.

England, I have one word for you: *FUCK YOU!!!!!!!!!!!!!!!!*

52

Watermelon Oreos: A Holocaust For The Metabolism

As much as I agree with my colleague Mr. Injustice that racism is one of the worst problems facing us as a society today, I must respectfully disagree that it is the very worst one.

As the saying goes, "You are what you eat," and what we are eating these days is shit.

Nabisco's new Watermelon Oreos may seem like innocent, fun, summertime treats, but they constitute just another log on the shitpile of the modern Western diet—the same diet that leads to racism, colon cancer, sexism, diabetes, classism, tooth decay, discrimination, and the wholesale slaughter of cows, chickens, poultry, and shellfish.

When I look at a Watermelon Oreo, I think—how many cows died to produce this cookie? How many cancer-causing sugars and food dyes went into this little Wafer of Death? How many children in the Third World will go to sleep hungry just so some fat fuck in Iowa can stuff his mouth with these Slabs of Sugary Shit during a midnight refrigerator raid?

The answer is, of course: TOO MANY.

The journey to the slaughterhouse only starts with one cookie.

Meat is murder. Bad diets lead to bad people. So as much as I agree with Mr. Injustice in principle, I believe he's putting the cart before the horse (not that I believe we should eat horse meat). Bad diets come first, *then* racism. Vegetarians don't lynch people. A vegetable never hurt anyone. Human beings are made of meat, which is why they kill.

53

I Ate a Hamburger—Should I Kill Myself?

When I'm wrong, I'm wrong, and this time I'm wrong. I mean, I've made it clear that when it comes to eating meat versus not eating meat—the biggest moral struggle currently facing us as a species—I'm on the good side of the battle. I will fight with my non-meat-eating friends on the front lines of a bloody crusade to ensure that not even a prepubescent hamster loses its life to fund the giant tentacles of Big Food and the Big Corporations that make Big Money to kill the little animals.

OK?

But last night I got really fucked up at a party—I mean, REALLY fucked up, like on eight or nine shots of Scotch, some pills, beer, some other pills, a bump to keep awake, then more pills—and went out wandering into the cold night.

And there, somewhere near 42nd Street, I looked through the steamy glass and saw a Greek man—OK, I'm assuming he's

Greek. He had dark hair and thick eyebrows and they serve those blue paper coffee cups with the Greek lettering, but beyond that, I should admit that I don't really know if he was Greek and it would be unfair to stereotype him—flipping burgers on a hot sizzlin' grill. Whether he was Greek or not really doesn't matter, does it?

So I walked in, ordered a hamburger, ate it, walked out, and I haven't been the same since.

Not to say the burger wasn't good. Of course it was good. That was the whole problem. I'm now a willing accomplice to the murder of a cow that was probably cut down in its prime, a cow that will never see its children graduate high school, a cow whose soul hovers over me, ever-ready and willing to take an invisible shit right on my head.

That cow is screaming right now as I type this. It's screaming from my stomach. Can you hear it? Press your ear closer to this book. Hear it? See what I mean?

I feel horrible about this, because it totally fucks up my cred among the other lacto-ovo-vegetarians. The vegans I don't really care about. Everyone knows they're crazy. But my whole circle consists of other "lacto-ovos," as we like to call ourselves.

I've thought about killing myself, but I'm not sure whether that would be the moral thing to do, or whether it would be piling one murder atop another and thereby really fucking up my karma in the process. At any given moment, I could go either way. It's like, half the time I'm all, "Linus—kill yourself—it's the right thing to do," and the other half I'm like, "Linus—don't kill yourself—that would be wrong."

Meanwhile, a dead cow moos out for vengeance and justice, preferably in that order. And there are some mighty big bloodstains on the hands of my soul.

54

Disgusting Fat Asshole Eats Burger, Has Heart Attack

Even though I seriously contemplated killing myself recently for eating a hamburger, I honestly and sincerely believe that God, who is probably a hermaphrodite but also possibly entirely female and has a clit the size of a baseball, spared me so I can continue calling for the live ritual murder and disembowelment of anyone who thinks it's "cute" or "cool" or "hip" or "snarky" to eat meat.

I have news for you: It isn't.

I don't know why I have to keep telling you this. It's probably because you're stupid. And evil. And selfish. And a serial killer. And a big A-hole on top of all that to boot.

But God(dess) has news for you, too, Mein Liebchen: There's a little thing called "karma." And if, by your actions, you endorse the mass herding, stun-gunning, murder, and oral consumption of cows, then karma will bite you as hard as some stupid asshole in Vegas recently bit into a burger called the "Triple Bypass" at a place called the Heart Attack Grill—AND THEN HAD A HEART ATTACK!

LOL LOL LOL LOL LOL LOL LOL LOL LOL LOL LOL LOL LOL LOL LOL LOL LOL LOL LOL LOL LOL LOL LOL LOL LOL LOL LOL LOL LOL LOL !!!!!!!!!!!!!!!!!!!!!

I laugh at your suffering, you animal-murderer. Now you know how it feels to be a cow. It doesn't feel good, does it?

The Heart Attack Grill also offers menu items such as "Butterfat Shakes" and "Flatliner Fries," all of them intended to be "jokes" that aren't funny at all because they're based upon a Holocaust of cow carcasses.

I hope everyone who eats there dies instantly. Seriously. Then maybe they'll learn something about a little thing I like to call "empathy."

55

Fat Woman's Corpse Sets Building Ablaze During Cremation

People who eat vegetables don't get fat. When their cadavers are set ablaze during the ancient and (in many cultures) sacred ritual of cremation, their corpses don't cause grease fires, either.

That's why I'm assuming a woman whose body set a building ablaze in Austria recently during a routine cremation must have been a meat-eater.

The disgusting hamburger-gobbling cow-killer tipped the scales at 440 pounds, which probably would have required a piano case or at least a refrigerator box if she wanted to be buried.

There was so much drippy yellow suet inside her bloated carcass that it actually caused a building fire when smaller and slimmer technicians, whom I'm assuming ate more vegetables and whole grains than she did, attempted to cremate her. Firefighters who arrived and brought the Inferno of Fat under control were said to be covered in "burnt grease."

Be right back...

OK, I vomited.

If she hadn't eaten so many innocent animals, this never would have happened. Like I said, I'm only assuming she was a meat-eater. But I know that when I get cremated, I'll go up in one sweet-smelling puff. And I won't have any bad karma that will cause me to be reborn as a cow who lives an unhappy life and is eventually murdered and then eaten. I'm better than all that.

56

If You Don't Boycott The All-White Academy Awards, You Deserve To Be Shot

Considering recent events in Ferguson, Staten Island, Cleveland—and, no doubt, coming to a town near you—one would hope that we, as a nation, are coming closer to achieving true racial harmony and equality.

Apparently the Academy of Motion Picture Arts & Sciences didn't get the memo.

The 2015 Oscars nominations are predictably, disgustingly white. All of the acting nominees are white. The beloved David Oyelowo, who turned in a stunning, tear-jerking portrayal of MLK in *Selma*, was left out in the cold.

David Oyelowo is a black man.

What sort of message does this send to our children?

It sends the message that white supremacy and institutional racism are still a thing.

"The lack of diversity in today's Oscar nominations is appalling," the Reverend Al Sharpton commented. "The movie industry is like the Rocky Mountains—the higher you get, the whiter it gets."

Remind me not to visit the Rocky Mountains, nor to purchase anything made in the Rocky Mountains, until justice is achieved.

Friends, allies, and comrades, I think we're going to climb that mountain one day. And believe you me, we're going to melt that snow. We're going to have an entertainment industry that reflects the horrors and degradation suffered by nonwhites and non-males throughout history, because that's the whole point of entertainment in the first place—it must teach, scold, inform, and uplift.

I have a blowtorch in one hand and a backpack full of bottled water and trail mix. Who's willing to climb that mountain with me?

57

I Feel That You Shouldn't Tell Me How I Should Feel About My Feelings

I agree with you that everyone's feelings are equal, but personally, I feel that my feelings should be more important to me than your feelings, no matter how you feel about it.

To be blunt—you might even call it unfeeling—I don't care how you feel about my feelings, even though I feel you'd say that I actually feel otherwise.

These are my feelings, not yours, and I'm owning them. I'm claiming them—or reclaiming them, that is. My feelings empower me, or at least that's the way I feel about it.

I acknowledge that your feelings are your feelings, not mine. That's undisputed, and it's not what we're arguing about, anyway. I honor and embrace that your feelings are your feelings, although

I also feel I should feel free to feel the way I want to feel about your feelings, whether in public or in private.

I hope you feel that I'm not trying to hurt your feelings, but I also feel that I should be honest with you and tell you that my feelings are personally more important to me than your feelings, and if you don't feel the same way, well, I guess that's the way you feel. Go ahead and feel hurt. I don't care.

If you want to feel that I'm not taking your feelings into account, that's fine—feel that way. I just wish you knew in your heart that that's not personally how I feel.

I believe in a "live and let live" mentality, which is why I feel that my rights to my feelings end right at the line where your feelings begin, almost as if we could draw territorial borders on Google Maps to demonstrate how truly separate your feelings and mine are.

One day I hope we feel the same way about this. Today is obviously not that day. So instead of letting you tell me how I should feel about things, I feel that we should spend the day apart, and maybe we'll feel different tonight—in other words, here's hoping that we both feel the same about this.

Anyway, I thought you should know how I feel. How do you feel about it? Not that I care.

Credits

*All articles were first published on thoughtcatalog.com in 2014 except
the following:*

Bay Aryan Resistance
(published in Filth *magazine, 1997)*

A Vast White-Wing Conspiracy
(published in New York Press, 1998)*

White Man Blames Women, Nonwhites For His Problems
Portland's White Community
Judge Orders Hitler To Undergo Therapy
(published in Exotic *magazine, 2002-2007)*

Torch Mobs For Tolerance
The Tolerance That Is Only Skin Deep
How To Deal With The Brainwashed
How The Free Speech Movement Stopped Moving
Land Of 1,000 Microaggressions
Arkansas Store Censors Elton John's Designer Baby!
The Importance Of Gender-Neutral Public Bathrooms For
Bisexual Space Aliens
The Shame Sham
What The Hell Do You Mean By "Social Justice," Anyway?
A Blizzard Of Special Snowflakes
(published on takimag.com from 2011-2016)

Criticizing PC Totalitarianism—A '90s Thing'?
(published on jimgoad.net, 2011)

Life Is Unfair, And I'm Here To Change That
Why The Fuck Are There No Gay Drivers In NASCAR?!?
Why Don't They Just Be Honest And Call It Rapebook?
The World's Most Racist Cereal
Social Justice Is Never Pleasant
This White Supremacist Fried Chicken Restaurant In Thailand
Is Clearly Unacceptable
Fabricated Hate Crimes By The Transgendered Are Still OK!!!
They're Already Misgendering The Royal Baby
*(published on streetcarnage.com under the pseudonym "Mr. Injustice,"
2012-2014)*

Watermelon Oreos: A Holocaust For The Metabolism
I Ate A Hamburger—Should I Kill Myself?
Disgusting Fat Asshole Eats Burger, Has Heart Attack
Fat Woman's Corpse Sets Building Ablaze During Cremation
*(published on streetcarnage.com under the pseudonym "Lacto-Ovo-Veg-
etarian Linus," 2012-2013)*

Made in the USA
Monee, IL
14 March 2021

62736541R00125